Gospel Brokenness

Gospel Brokenness

The Unexpected Path to Deep Joy

CLAY WERNER

WIPF & STOCK · Eugene, Oregon

GOSPEL BROKENNESS
The Unexpected Path to Deep Joy

Copyright © 2019 Clay Werner. All rights reserved. Except for brief quotations in critical publications or reviews, no part of this book may be reproduced in any manner without prior written permission from the publisher. Write: Permissions, Wipf and Stock Publishers, 199 W. 8th Ave., Suite 3, Eugene, OR 97401.

Wipf & Stock
An Imprint of Wipf and Stock Publishers
199 W. 8th Ave., Suite 3
Eugene, OR 97401

www.wipfandstock.com

PAPERBACK ISBN: 978-1-5326-8543-9
HARDCOVER ISBN: 978-1-5326-8544-6
EBOOK ISBN: 978-1-5326-8545-3

Manufactured in the U.S.A.   11/20/19

Unless otherwise indicated, all Scripture quotations are from The Holy Bible, English Standard Version, copyright © 2001 by Crossway Bibles, a division of Good News Publishers. Used by permission. All rights reserved.

To Hilary and Jenny,
For the gift of God's word in '99.

To Ryan Misbach,
For teaching me to treasure God's word in DeHority Hall.

Contents

Acknowledgments | ix
Introduction | xi

1. Reading Psalm 32 with a Psalm-shaped Heart | 1
2. A Blessed Heart | 14
3. A Transparent Heart | 27
4. An Exhausted Heart | 40
5. A Confessing Heart | 53
6. An Inviting Heart | 67
7. A Wise Heart | 78
8. A Joyful Heart | 91
9. The Path Towards Deep Joy: Gospel Brokenness | 101

Bibliography | 113

Acknowledgments

I've dedicated this book to three people who have greatly impacted my life. Hilary and Jenny Webb have been good friends throughout my life but were crucial to my coming to faith in Christ just prior to leaving for college. For my high school graduation, they bought me the gift of a Bible with my name inscribed on the front. God used that Bible to give me new life and a driving passion for God's word. Hilary and Jenny, thank you for the gift that forever changed me.

I've also dedicated it to my friend Ryan Misbach. We met my freshmen year at Ball State University in Muncie, Indiana, and he patiently helped me understand how to read Scripture as we initially walked our way through Romans. It was in that time, as we navigated Romans 4, that I was introduced to Psalm 32. Ryan, your friendship through the years has been and always will be a tremendous gift to me.

My wife, Liz, and our children Isaac, Claire, David, Andrew, and Noah, all deserve special mention. As I began to write this, I had an accident and completely tore my Achilles tendon. For three months they waited on me faithfully as I couldn't walk anywhere and was expected to remain as still as possible while recovering from surgery. They were a gracious embodiment to me of God's patient love and servant heart.

I'm also grateful for the team at Wipf and Stock and the opportunity to publish with them. They've been a tremendous help and an encouragement along the way to get this book in your hands.

Introduction

ALL OF OUR HEARTS, whether we know it or not, long to know the deep joy of possessing and experiencing the permanent and passionate favor of God. However, all of our hearts also experience the twisted desires of sin and the foolish bent towards trying to deal with it in our own strength, which usually means somehow trying to cover it up so others, especially God, won't see. This two-step dance of struggling and covering leaves us exhausted and more hardened. Everyone who knows Christ knows about this tiring battle.

However, the gospel is so extravagant that even a king like David, who sinned and tried to hide it, can find immeasurable and unexpected grace that restores spiritual vitality and makes one a wise counselor of mercy to the surrounding community. Everyone who knows Christ also has this hope and is invited to experience again the superabundant grace found in this remarkably rich section of the Psalms.

This book is an invitation to explore the treasures of grace found in Psalm 32. This psalm is a personal and powerful poem that seeks to redirect our hearts to the truest and deepest source of joy while also transforming us through the incomparable power of God's saving and transforming grace.

Psalm 32 is personal. In this psalm you'll see that not only is King David speaking to you with brutally honest transparency, but God himself is addressing you and inviting you to come home and be embraced in his love and experience the feast of his grace. Because of this, Psalm 32 was Augustine's favorite psalm. He had it

INTRODUCTION

read to him frequently and even had it inscribed on the wall next to his sickbed in order to be comforted by it.[1] I came to cherish Psalm 32 in college when a friend pointed me to it after I confessed struggles with sin and a desire to feel the comforting assurance of the gospel. I meditate on it frequently and use it regularly when I speak at other churches or groups. John Owen, a theological hero of mine, regularly encouraged pastors to speak only on what they had experienced personally. In the pages that follow, I hope you can sense that it has been an anchor in my own life and that I share with you some of what I know from the treasures of its truth.

Psalm 32 is also powerful. For centuries God's people have turned to this psalm to be motivated and empowered to turn from sin and turn toward God. As you'll see, it has the power to change our mind's focused attention, our heart's deepest affections, and our life's greatest devotion as it points us to the very heart of God. It is a living and active word that can both wound and heal, convict and comfort. My prayer is that you'll open your heart to receive its wisdom.

Psalm 32 shows us the unexpected path to deep joy: gospel brokenness. This phrase comes from Scotty Smith and Steven Curtis Chapman's book *Restoring Broken Things*. They make a helpful distinction between the brokenness that sin creates in our lives and the brokenness that we feel and experience over our sin. In our current evangelical culture, the language of brokenness can be used to avoid the language of sin, but I want to use the phrase "gospel brokenness" as an explanation of how we should respond to our sin in repentance. I do think, however, that people inside the church often assume they know what repentance is and that people outside the church often have deep misconceptions about it. There are a variety of reasons for this.

First, we are all swimming in a culture that allows for and even encourages a tailor-made morality. What is wrong or right for one person isn't wrong or right for another. The greatest sin seems to be if someone claims that some action is actually a sin. Second, inside and outside the church the concept of sin is understood

---

1. See Craigie and Tate, *Psalms 1–50*, 268.

INTRODUCTION

superficially to consist primarily of, if not solely, actions. A deeper understanding of it as coming from the corruption of our hearts and having a lingering disposition towards waywardness is missing in many of our churches. Third, we overestimate our own goodness and strength. In other words, rather than needing rescue from the great power of sin, we only need some self-help tips to improve our lives.

Gospel brokenness seeks to enable a fresh hearing of what the work of repentance in the life of a believer can and should look like. As David mentions in Psalm 51, God will not despise a broken spirit and a contrite heart; rather, he will renew the joy of their salvation. Smith and Chapman encourage this gospel brokenness,

> because only the gospel of God's grace can enable us to be completely honest about our stuff without falling into toxic shame or self-contempt. And only the gospel can humble us, soften us, and give us the power to repent—or, at least, not run away or rant. When followers of Jesus walk openly in this kind of brokenness—*gospel brokenness*—angels in heaven rejoice, and people without faith, or those with much cynicism about Christians, are likely to reconsider who Jesus is.
>
> Write this down: no greater beauty can be found at *any point* or in *any place* in God's Story than the times when God's people manifest this *gospel brokenness*—for that's where God's glory is revealed most clearly.[2]

This book seeks to help you along in the journey of knowing gospel brokenness and experiencing the deepest joy that it brings as you walk through Psalm 32.

However, no matter how many words are used to write this book, I still cannot do better than the concise language of the *Westminster Shorter Catechism*:

> What is repentance unto life?
>
> Repentance unto life is a saving grace, whereby a sinner, out of a true sense of his sin, and apprehension of the mercy of God in Christ, doth, with grief and hatred of

---

2. Smith and Chapman, *Restoring Broken Things*, 66–67 (emphasis theirs).

INTRODUCTION

his sin, turn from it unto God, with full purpose of, and endeavor after, new obedience.[3]

Resources like the Westminster Confession, along with the works of men like John Owen, Richard Sibbes, John Calvin, Jack Miller, and many others, have helped me along this path of gospel brokenness that I'm still walking on. You'll notice their fingerprints throughout these pages.

May the joy of the Lord be your strength as you walk with me through Psalm 32 in what lies ahead.

---

3. *Westminster Shorter Catechism*, Question 87.

1

Reading Psalm 32 with a Psalm-shaped Heart

POETRY OFTEN HAS A unique ability to penetrate more deeply into the human heart than mere statements of fact. This is why, in Scripture, God is portrayed not only as the King of kings and Lord of lords, but also as the Poet of poets in the psalms. In fact, if you were to gather up all of the poetry in the entire Bible, it would be longer than the New Testament. God could have delivered a systematic theology of revealed truth to our doorstep, but instead he communicates through the complex history of family and national narratives, the deep insight of wisdom, passionate and personal letters, apocalyptic visions, and stirring poetry that conveys an anatomy of all the parts of our souls.[1] The intentional target at which the poetry of the psalms is pointed, is the core of who we are.

---

1. This last comment on poetry comes from Calvin's comments in his introduction to Psalms. See Janz and Jordon, *Reformation Reader*, 205.

Gospel Brokenness

Poetry's Target Is the Heart

While we must use our minds rigorously to understand the psalms, their purpose is to penetrate our defenses and hit us where it counts: in the heart. Old Testament scholar Tremper Longman says that poetry has the "unique power to reach deep into our souls and move us in a way that largely bypasses the rational and speaks directly to our hearts."[2]

When the psalms speak, they speak from the heart. This is why Jesus said, "out of the abundance of the heart, the mouth speaks" (Luke 6:45). Words, then, not only reveal who we are, but what condition our heart is in. When the psalmists speak, they are declaring the heart of the writer, whether it be a season of joyful praise, mournful lament, or humble confession. Yet, the ultimate Author of the psalms is God, who inspired the authors in their writing so that they wouldn't only reveal human hearts, but also the divine heart of God. Not only has God spoken in the psalms, but he continues to speak—present-tense—every time we peruse their pages and immerse our souls in their verses.[3] As you read Psalm 32, God is directly and personally speaking to you.

Thus, the poetry of the psalms communicates the heart of God. The psalms are filled with human language stretched to its farthest capacity in order to capture the sweeping panoramic vision of the beauty of God's being and character. Not only is his being "from everlasting to everlasting" (41:13), but so also is his steadfast love (103:17). He dwells in the highest heavens but hears the groans of the lowliest prisoner, setting him free (102:19–20). His power is unparalleled (106:8) and his justice is perfect (9:7–8). He is "merciful and gracious, slow to anger and abounding in steadfast love and faithfulness" (86:15). The psalms captivate our hearts with the way they portray the glory of God.

They also communicate the heart of his people. They valiantly put their trust in God even when surrounded by countless and

---

2. Longman, *Reading the Bible*, 115.

3. This comes out clearly whenever the author of the book of Hebrews quotes a psalm and uses the present tense verb of "say."

vicious enemies (25:2). They are confident that God, in his faithfulness, will fulfill his purposes for them (71:21), they are faithful in their pursuit of God's ways (119:30), and are filled with liturgies of praise for all God has done (150). Yet, they are also filled at times with drowning sorrow, confused by God's seeming absence (42:3). They sin grievously (51) and wander repeatedly (119:67, 176). They groan in exhaustion and frustration in the midst of incomprehensible suffering (88:3–6). The psalms invite and draw our hearts closer to them with the way they realistically portray the everyday inner lives of those who place their faith in God.

So, whether they are portraying God's heart or expressing the heart of the believer, the psalms are teaching us wisdom in "the secret heart" (51:6).

There are a variety of ways that Scripture in general, and the psalms in particular, teach us to engage the psalms, but we will focus on four principles that are most important as we seek to consider Psalm 32. The psalms themselves teach us to approach Psalm 32 by seeking God with our whole heart, listening to God with a meditative heart, relying on God with a humble heart, and asking God for a transformed heart.

Seeking God with Our Whole Heart

Herbert Simon, a Nobel Prize-winning psychologist and economist, once said, "A wealth of information creates poverty of attention."[4] We struggle with many things in the twenty-first century, but at the beginning of 2020, we all struggle with poverty of attention. We are distracted and divided. MIT Professor and author Sherry Turkle has shown that almost every person is on a spectrum from intermittently to completely distracted at any given moment, especially by technology.[5] Alan Noble says that our culture is seeking to train us to insatiably pursue the next tweet, next job, next comment, next gathering, next anything at hyper speed,

---

4. Quoted in Goleman, *Focus*, 9.
5. Turkle, *Reclaiming Conversation*, 108.

often leaving us frayed and exhausted.⁶ Even the psalmist in Psalm 119 acknowledges how prone his heart is to wander (119:10).

We don't, however, wander into distraction simply because of noise outside of us, but also because of the clamor of divided desires within our hearts. Sin hates exposure when we draw near to God, so it will seek to capture our attention with anything to keep us from seeking him wholeheartedly. Want to pray? Yes, but you're tired from being with the kids and you missed that episode you wanted to watch last night and Netflix is calling your name. Want to read your Bible? Yes, but how can you when your roommate was so thoughtless, borrowed your iPad, and broke it? Feeding thoughts of bitterness feels pretty inviting. From the mildly trivial to the obviously sinful, the sin in our heart is eagerly strategizing against us to keep us away from the transforming presence of God.

In the midst of the distractedness of our lives and the dividedness of our hearts, the psalms call us to the inner sanctuary to seek and enjoy the face of God.⁷ In Psalm 27:4, David says,

> One thing have I asked of the LORD, that will I seek after: that I may dwell in the house of the LORD all the days of my life, to gaze upon the beauty of the LORD and to inquire in his temple.

He later prays, "You have said, 'Seek my face.' My heart says to you, 'Your face, LORD, do I seek'" (Ps 27:8).

Rather than David's "one thing" being for God to take away personal dangers or circumstantial difficulties, he prays for spiritual intimacy, nearness to the heart of God. In fact, he prays to get so near that he would see God's face and gaze on the beauty of his glory. Later, Psalm 119 pronounces a blessing on those who seek God with their whole heart (v. 2). The psalmist then states "With my whole heart I seek you" (v. 10).

We zealously seek what we personally value, that's why Jesus said, "where your treasure is, there your heart will be also" (Matt 6:21). Seeking God in the psalms means that we are seeking his

---

6. Noble, *Disruptive Witness*, 14.
7. Longman, *How to Read the psalms*, 11–12, 57.

presence as the greatest treasure we could ever desire. Seeking God wholeheartedly means that we seek him with a mind singularly focused on the pursuit and a heart undividedly given to what will most deeply satisfy us. In his face you behold the soul-satisfying beauty of glory and from his heart you experience fullness of joy and pleasures forevermore (Ps 24:10; 16:11). This should be your grace-fueled passion as you read, study, and meditate on Psalm 32.

Listening to God with a Meditative Heart

Seeking God with our whole heart means opening the pages of the psalms and finding God in his inner sanctuary, eager to meet with us. Yet, when we open these pages and read the poetry of these psalms, what are we to do? Meditate.

We not only seek what we value, as mentioned above, but we consistently think about and ruminate on what we value. Think about the middle-schooler who is certain he met his one true love, the college student whose life dream is to produce her own Broadway show, the lawyer who wants to make partner in her firm. Their hearts are consumed with the object of their desires and dreams. Let's think of something else people often consider—priceless works of art.

Dr. James Elkins is the chair of art history, theory, and criticism at the School of the Art Institute of Chicago. He has dedicated his career to training artists and helping others understand how to appreciate works of art. In an article written for the *Huffington Post*, he encourages the reader to refrain from the common temptation to simply glance at a work of art only to walk on to the next piece:

> What I have in mind is a different kind of experience: not just glancing, but looking, staring, gazing, sitting or standing transfixed: forgetting, temporarily, the errands you have to run, or the meeting you're late for, and thinking, living, only inside the work. Falling in love with an

artwork, finding that you somehow need it, wanting to return to it, wanting to keep it in your life.[8]

In other words, you will not genuinely grasp the meaning of the painting nor discern its value unless you look, stare, gaze, and stand transfixed by it. It is a visual treasure that demands our undivided attention, repetitive visitation, and thoughtful consideration.

The psalmists consider God's word a treasure, and not simply a treasure, but the greatest treasure (Ps 119:127, 162; 19:10). One of the many reasons that it is a treasure is because in it, not only do we read that God *has spoken* in the psalms, but he *continues to speak* to us as we ponder their truth.[9]

A heart shaped by the psalms has learned the value of God's word and the value of meditating on God's word. But the question remains: What does it mean to meditate? Psalm 1, considered the doorway to the psalms, is important here. It states that the person is blessed who delights in God's word and meditates on it (v. 2). In its use of parallelism, a tool of the psalms where the second statement uses similar language to the first and builds on it, it implies that meditation entails delight. One can either meditate *because* they delight in God's word or *in order to* delight in God's word.[10]

The psalmist also mentions that we are to meditate on God's word "day and night" (Ps 1:2). This entails the regular repetition of considering the truth of the psalm. If, then, I were to venture to define meditation using my own words, I might say that meditation is repetitively considering and consuming God's truth in order to commune with, delight in, and be changed by God.[11]

---

8. Elkins, "How Long Does it Take?," para. 7.

9. It is surely for this point that the author of Hebrews almost always cites a psalm or some other portion of the Old Testament by saying that the Holy Spirit "says" (present tense).

10. See also Psalm 119:14–16, 47, 97.

11. To change metaphors from painting, Isaiah 31:4 describes a lion slowly devouring its prey and uses the imagery that the lion is "growling" (same word Ps 1:2 uses for meditate!). It is slowly eating and enjoying every morsel before it's all gone. For more on the psalms and meditating, see Futato, *Transformed by Praise*, 92–97; Godfrey, *Learning to Love the Psalms*, 15. See Clowney, *Christian Meditation*.

Reading Psalm 32 with a Psalm-shaped Heart

To read Psalm 32 with a psalm-shaped heart, it should be approached repetitively and considerately, with the purpose of fellowshiping with God, enjoying his presence, and being transformed by his grace. As Dr. Elkins encouraged, sit in front of Psalm 32 looking, staring, gazing, and standing transfixed.

Relying on God with a Humble Heart

Up to this point, we've seen that the psalms command us to come to them wholeheartedly seeking God and meditatively listening to God. While this is helpful, it's not the whole picture. The larger picture of Scripture is what Martin Luther and other Reformers taught as the crucial distinction between law and gospel.

While telling us to wholeheartedly seek God, the psalms also tell us that there is *no one who seeks God* left to themselves (Ps 14:2; see also Rom 3:11). Their commands to seek God are laws that we cannot, but should, obey. We are naturally distracted away from God and his word in a thousand different directions and for innumerable reasons. We are naturally divided in our hearts, giving into various trivial or sinful desires.

The gospel is that through Christ's life, death, and resurrection, God gives *regenerating grace* to us so that we will actually seek him in the gospel. If we find our hearts seeking him and seeking his word, it is because he has given us a new heart (Ezek 36:26). The psalms also declare that God is joyfully willing to give us *enabling grace* so that we can seek him with our whole hearts and meditate on his word. This is why the psalmist, in total dependence on God, cries out, "Incline my heart to your word" (119:36, 112)! The humble heart, then, acknowledges its complete spiritual inability and depends on God completely for regenerating and enabling grace.

The command to meditate on God's word is also law. We're like Americans that visit the Louvre. Stocked with many of the world's most highly celebrated and priceless artifacts from centuries of craftsmanship, studies have shown that the average person stands in front of a priceless piece of art for less than three seconds.[12] They stand in front of the ancient code of Hammurabi and think, "Oh, that's nice. Next!" They stand in front of Delecroix's "Liberty Leading the People" and say, "That's nice. Next!" Michelangelo, same thing. *The Mona Lisa*, however, is different. She gets a whopping thirteen seconds per visitor.

These untrained visitors don't know the value of what is in front of them, so they keep on looking for something else. That is what our hearts often do with the beauty displayed in Scripture. We may look at it briefly, claim that it is nice, and then keep on looking for the next thing. Our hearts, not our eyes, haven't been trained to see the incredible value of Scripture in general, and of Christ crucified in particular. The gospel, however, opens our eyes to see the value of Scripture and meditate on its truth. This is the cry of the psalmist, again in dependence on God: "Open my eyes, that I may behold wondrous things out of your law" (Ps 119:18; see also Eph 1:17–18).[13] The gospel gives us this *illuminating grace* as the Spirit unfolds for us the beauty of God's heart in Scripture.

Last, the humble heart is given both the *graces of exposure and healing*. God's word is like a sword that cuts into us, showing what is genuinely inside (Heb 3:11–12). It exposes our deceit, our sin, our waywardness. It also gives healing, bringing renewal to the areas that have been exposed.[14]

The heart that approaches Psalm 32 must come with a willingness to be exposed, to be healed, to be renewed, and to cry out with Augustine's prayer, "Lord, command what you will, and give what you command!"[15]

---

12. See Elkins, "How Long Does it Take?"

13. "Law" is used in this verse not for the narrow sense of "command," but for the broader sense of "instruction" throughout God's word.

14. See especially Johnson, "One Edge of a Two-Edged Sword."

15. Quoted in Trueman, *Grace Alone*, 58.

Reading Psalm 32 with a Psalm-shaped Heart

Praying for a Transformed Heart

Psalm 119 says that the purpose of meditating on and storing up God's word in our heart is so that we might not sin again him (v. 11) and that we might keep our way pure (v. 9). Sadly, part of the sickness of the human heart is that apart from God's grace, we live for ourselves (2 Cor 5:15; Phil 2:21). God's word, however, helps us to reorient our lives Godward in worship. This is crucial because what we need most is not behavior management but worship re-alignment. I like to consider worship as giving God our mind's focused attention, our heart's deepest affection, and our life's greatest devotion. Let's look at these.

First, the psalms help us worship God by focusing our mind's attention on his glory and goodness. Consider Psalm 24. Towards the end of the psalm, its constant refrain is "Who is this King of glory" that is entering the gates? It creates anticipation with our minds as we seek the arrival of this glorious King. Psalm 107 gives us snapshots of the various ways God expresses his steadfast love to those who trust him. While the concerns of an average day or even sin may cause our attention to wander, the psalms invite us to worship God by drawing our mind's attention back to the glory and faithfulness of our God and King.

Second, God uses the psalms to transform our heart's affection. As Augustine, Luther, C. S. Lewis, and many others have pointed out, the natural condition of our hearts is that our loves are disordered. We often love too much what is actually trivial and love too little what is enormously meaningful. Though not a Christian, David Foster Wallace was right:

> There is no such thing as not worshipping. Everybody worships. The only choice we get is what to worship. And the compelling reason for maybe choosing some sort of god or spiritual-type thing to worship . . . is that pretty much anything else you worship will eat you alive.[16]

---

16. Wallace, *This Is Water*, 99.

Wallace is saying what Psalm 115 and 135 declare—that those who worship idols become like them. God uses the psalms, then, to reorient our love toward what is truly lovely—himself.

The psalms not only change what we focus on and what we love, but they also transform our life's devotion. We pursue with passion whatever we love. Like a deer pants after water, so our souls should pant after God (Ps 42:1). In the desert of life, where there is no life-sustaining water or food, we pursue God as the feast of our souls (Ps 63:1–4). Not just our mind, not just our hearts, but our entire lives, every sphere and season, are oriented around seeking, pursuing, and knowing our gracious God.

As we approach Psalm 32 together, we should ask God in prayer to realign every fiber of our being around knowing and worshiping him.

Knowing the Heart of God

Seeking God with a whole heart, listening to God with a meditative heart, relying on God with a humble heart, and asking God for a transformed heart all combine to move us toward our one aim—knowing the heart of God.

Author Os Guinness has insightfully written that all of us carry around inaccurate and inadequate views of God that sometimes lead us to doubt his goodness.[17] Inaccurate means that we believe something wrong about him; inadequate means that what we believe is true but not yet fully grasping the enormity and beauty of his nature and glory.

Psalm 73 is a psalm where the author was gripped with an inadequate and inaccurate perception of God. He begins envying the wealthy, regretting his faithfulness to the Lord when he could've been pursuing more tangible, even sinful, means of satisfaction. Yet, when he "went into the sanctuary of God" (v. 17) he was confronted with the consequences of a godless life. He also rediscovered the knowledge of God as good (v. 1), as a strong refuge (v. 28),

---

17. Guinness, *God in the Dark*, 57–74.

and as his forever portion (v. 26). This abiding in God's sanctuary changed the psalmist's life.

Meeting God in the sanctuary of the psalms replaces our erroneous views of God with truth and our inadequate views of God with more adequate views.[18] This is essential for our understanding of repentance in Psalm 32. One of the ways sin keeps us away from God is to disfigure the truth about God's heart toward sinners. Yes, God is a judge, but as we'll see, he is not only a judge. He is willing and eager to show steadfast love toward wayward prodigals. Put another way, he delights to show an abundance of steadfast love toward those who have sinned (Ps 147:10–11; 69:13). It is in truly knowing God that we will begin to genuinely turn from sin.

Looking at and Looking Along

Let me end this chapter with an experience of C. S. Lewis in a toolshed, which will help explain how we are going to navigate Psalm 32:

> I was standing today in the dark toolshed. The sun was shining outside and through the crack at the top of the door there came a sunbeam. From where I stood that beam of light, with the specks of dust floating in it, was the most striking thing in the place. Everything else was almost pitch-black. I was seeing the beam, not seeing things by it.
>
> Then I moved, so that the beam fell on my eyes. Instantly the whole previous picture vanished. I saw no toolshed, and (above all) no beam. Instead I saw, framed in the irregular cranny at the top of the door, green leaves moving on the branches of a tree outside and beyond that, 90 odd million miles away, the sun. *Looking along the beam, and looking at the beam are very different experiences.*[19]

---

18. While we should strive to grow in the knowledge of God's heart and grace, we can never call our knowledge of him "adequate" because he is infinite.

19. Lewis, *God in the Dock*, 230 (emphasis mine).

We will look *at* Psalm 32 and seek to better understand its historical, cultural, and grammatical context. However, we will also take a cue from Jesus when he gave his disciples a personal Bible study after the resurrection and showed them that the law of Moses, the Prophets, and the psalms all pointed to him (Luke 24:44). Thus, we'll also look *along* Psalm 32 and see how it points us toward, and portrays for us in advance, the person and work of our Savior, Jesus Christ.

Now we're ready to begin our journey as we listen to the Poet of poets speak through the poet David, "the sweet psalmist of Israel" (2 Sam 23:1).

Chapter Summary

Poetry, which comprises an enormous amount of Scripture, targets our hearts. The poetry of the psalms communicates and reveals both the heart of God and the heart of the psalmist in order to teach us wisdom. There are four main ways they challenge us to approach them. First, amidst the distraction and division of our heart, they challenge us to seek God with our whole heart. Next, they encourage us to listen to God with a meditative heart, increasingly learning the value and depth of God's word. Third, they call us to rely on God with a humble heart, realizing that any movement toward, or worship of, God is a gift of God's grace to us. Last, we should approach the psalms while praying for a transformed heart, asking that God enable us to focus our mind's attention, heart's affection, and life's devotion completely on him. These four movements will enable us to grow in knowing God's heart more accurately and adequately, especially as he is most climactically revealed in Christ.

Study Questions

1. What are things that you are aware of that might distract you as you seek to focus your heart on the treasure of Psalm 32?

2. Why is it important that God speaks to us in Scripture through various genres, but especially in poetry?

3. What specific areas of your life do you want to see God transform as you walk through this study?

2

A Blessed Heart

> Blessed is the one whose transgression is forgiven, whose sin is covered. Blessed is the man against whom the LORD counts no iniquity, and in whose spirit there is no deceit.
>
> PSALM 32:1–2

IF YOU HAVE SERIOUS issues with your heart, it is helpful to have the best surgeons around to care for you. On a chilly morning in 1685, King Charles II was sitting in his barber's chair when he unexpectedly fell over. While he didn't know it at the time, his heart was beginning to fail. Immediately, fourteen of the top English physicians of the day and a few wizards—yes, even a few wizards—began to attend to him in order to restore his health. Needless to say, their methods may have caused the king a little pain.

First, they made some incisions which let out enough blood to fill a large Coke bottle. They then made three enormous cuts into his shoulders. Why? To let out the poison that was invading his heart of course! With cuts all over, they made him smell various things that would induce vomiting while simultaneously using animal bladders to inject him with various leaves, flowers, cinnamon, and rock salt. They made him drink enormous amounts of absinthe. Finally, saving the best for last, they rubbed bird droppings on his feet and dead flies on his bald head. I'm sure that last one was in the latest medical journal of the day. "If ever there was a Monty Pythonesque attempt to prevent death, this was it. . . . Alas, all of the king's men could not put him together again."[1]

If it isn't obvious yet, the king of England didn't make it and you and I should be glad that cardiology has made a few improvements since the time of King Charles II.

Psalm 32 is about another king with different heart problems. This king's problems go even deeper and deal with more ultimate realities than the little fist-sized blood-pumping machine we all have in our chests. His problems are with his spiritual heart, a reality on which the Bible has more than a little to say. While we don't actually know the specific sin or sins that David is talking about, it's clear that he had sinned in some way and tried for a season to deal with it on his own, bringing about great damage to his own heart. This psalm is his reflection on what he had done and how God dealt with him while also being a mirror into our own heart and a window into God's.[2]

Bless Your Heart

David begins by declaring certain people "blessed." I grew up in southern Indiana, but have been in the southeastern part of the United States for a good season now. I've realized, over time, that the word "bless" has many connotations in the South. It can be the nice kid working at the fast-food restaurant who tells you to have "a blessed day"—which means "I have to say this to everyone because

---

1. Monagan and Williams, *Journey into the Heart*, 5–6.
2. It's important to consider this psalm in contrast to Psalm 51. Psalm 51 was more than likely written briefly after David's encounter with the prophet Nathan in 2 Sam 12, when his emotions were raw and his heart was in a spiritual vortex. In Psalm 32, we seem to be receiving truth that has been experienced, walked through, considered, meditated on, and now lovingly shared with others for our benefit.

my manager demands it or I lose my job. Here's your burger." It can be the incredibly jovial older woman after church that wishes you to have "a blessed week"—by which she means "I sincerely hope you have a week filled with great circumstances and good people and absent of any hardship." I've also realized that people who are very busy use it a lot to basically say, "I'm busy. This conversation is over. But I have to go and I don't want to be impolite. So, blessings."

Despite some of its cultural trappings, the word "bless" is rich with meaning. Translating it as "happy"[3] or "happy estate"[4] is legitimate, but this still leaves the term too vague. While it can result in a subjective state of happiness inside a believer, it actually conveys an objective status on those who have faith in Christ.[5] First, it means that those who trust in Christ objectively possess God's favor. Their standing in God's eyes has changed in light of God's grace. They've gone from orphans to adopted children; from alienated to brought near; from guilty to forgiven. All of this because of God's grace. Secondly, it also means "flourishing."[6] In other words, now that God is their Father and they've been united to Christ, their hearts can spiritually flourish even when their circumstances don't.[7] This indeed should result in being happy. Perhaps if we took a stab at defining it in a way that conveys more of the word's rich texture, we might say that "blessing" is the deep joy of possessing

---

3. Kidner, *Psalms 1–72*, 133.

4. Craigie and Tate, *Psalms 1–50*, 266.

5. Remember, David is situated historically in the Old covenant, the blessings of which are outlined in Deuteronomy 28. Though those blessings were ways in which God showed his favor, they looked forward to the time when Jesus would both bear the covenant curses on behalf of law-breakers and faithfully obey the law on their behalf. In light of this, the new covenant pronounces that the Father has "blessed us in Christ with every spiritual blessing" (Eph 1:3). These blessings cannot be taken away as they stand on a better, everlasting covenant. These blessings also flow to us through our union with Christ by faith. As I will discuss later, one of the primary "blessings" that Paul takes from this text in Romans 4 is justification.

6. Pennington, *Sermon on the Mount*, 41–68.

7. Although complete and final blessedness will entail the renewal of heaven and earth and the removal of all sin and suffering.

and experiencing God's passionate and permanent favor in our lives.

Searching for Little "b" Blessing

Biblically speaking, then, our hearts are most deeply happy when we are blessed by God, knowing his favor and having hearts that flourish in union with Christ. Yet sadly, with our heart's remaining corruption, we still struggle with looking for happiness—living waters—somewhere else (Jer 2:13). This is exactly what David had done. He had sought the "little b" blessing of some kind of idolatrous relationship, substance, or experience. And it worked, at least for a season. Remember, even the Bible admits that sin can be pleasurable (Heb 11:25) in the beginning, but corrupting and devastating in its impact on our hearts in the end. Giving into sinful desires distracts us and numbs us to our deeper hunger to have our greatest desire fulfilled—to have fellowship with, and be blessed by, God himself.

Never Expecting Blessing

Not only does pursuing ultimate happiness through horizontal means fail, but shame also keeps us from experiencing the blessedness or happiness of this psalm. The only thing shame requires to exist is a pulse. Whether or not you realize it, everyone deals with shame to one extent or another.[8] Shame is a sense or a feeling of not just doing something wrong, but of being deeply flawed and permanently unlovable. Not only does shame fear disconnection from others, it actually causes disconnection because it never opens up for fear of exposure. As Edward Welch comments, "You are on the sidelines and everyone else is in the game. You are off in the shadows while your friends are on the dance floor."[9] It's both a prison we can't escape and a home we never want to leave. It

---

8. See Welch, *Shame Interrupted,* and Thompson, *Soul of Shame.*
9. Welch, *Shame Interrupted,* 30.

pre-programs us to avoid hope and encouragement. It is a squatter that never leaves, a resistant virus to everything we treat it with, it is life-dominating and stubborn.[10] In other words, shame silently convinces our hearts that we can never experience God's blessing because of something we've done, something someone has done to us, or simply by being who we are.

Whether we think blessing consists of horizontal enjoyments and prosperity, or that we're so bad that we'll never experience the joy of God's blessing, the psalm invites us to ask the question as we continue: Whose heart does God bless? To whom does he give his passionate and permanent favor?

Bless Whose Heart?

Our Default DNA

A few years ago, Johns Hopkins University sent an email to almost 300 of its 1,800 applicants for admission. The title of the email, sent on a Friday afternoon, contained the subject line, "Embrace the YES" and went on to welcome each student "as one of the new members of the family." These students had studied, practiced, and performed almost perfectly in their academics and extracurricular activities in their high school years and now their dreams were coming true. They put the news of their acceptance on social media while many of their excited families threw extravagant parties. There was no end to their enthusiasm and expectation for the bright future that was directly in front of them.

Or so they thought.

On the following Sunday afternoon those same 300 students received another email from the prestigious university stating that they had been rejected and that the university had made a "technical mistake." As the Vice Provost of Admissions stated, "We very much regret having added to the disappointment felt by a group of very capable and hardworking students."[11] The students

---

10. Welch, *Shame Interrupted*, 12.
11. Anderson, "Johns Hopkins Mistakenly Says 'Yes,'" para. 12.

A Blessed Heart

were capable and hardworking, just not capable and hardworking *enough* to be joyfully welcomed into the Johns Hopkins family.

The default DNA of our hearts is to think that we must somehow perform well enough to earn God's blessing and favor. Sadly, this default sometimes digs deeper ruts in our hearts through our relationship with our parents or various life experiences. *New York Times* opinion writer and award-winning author David Brooks calls this "directional love":

> Children are bathed in love, but it is often directional love. Parents shower their kids with affection, but it is meritocratic affection. It is intermingled with the desire to help their children achieve worldly success.[12]

Very frequently it is manipulative. Parents unconsciously shape their smiles and frowns to steer their children toward behavior they think will lead to achievement. Parents glow with extra fervor when their child studies hard, practices hard, wins first place, or gets into a prestigious college. As Brooks goes on to note:

> This sort of love is merit based. It is not simply: I love you. It is, I love you when you stay on my balance beam. I shower you with praise and care when you're on my beam.[13]

We're convinced that we'll be blessed if we stay on God's balance beam. The blessed, those who possess and experience God's passionate and permanent favor, are those who always say please and thank you, never miss an event at church, dress modestly and watch conservative news, get up at the crack of dawn to read their Bibles, don't listen to the radio but pray while they drive to work, never lust after someone and only watch Hallmark movies, and have heroes like Billy Graham and Mother Theresa rather than Kim Kardashian. You get the picture—you only get a note from God saying "Embrace the BLESS" and "Welcome to the family" if you're on his moral balance beam.

---

12. Brooks, "Love and Merit," para. 3.
13. Brooks, "Love and Merit," para. 5.

Gospel Brokenness

The Surprise of Grace

Psalm 32, however, speaks into the default mode of our hearts and surprises us with its grace. It pronounces as blessed those who have sin, iniquity, and transgressions still lurking far below the surface. In their lives, they have sinned. Sin is that missing of the mark where God calls us to a certain standard and we fall woefully short of it. We miss the mark of loving God with our whole heart, soul, mind, and body, and loving our neighbors as ourselves. We miss the mark with daily opportunities to care for the needs of others and tend to their hearts. We miss the mark as we consider our needs most important and our time most valuable. But the grace of being blessed is only reserved for those who have sinned.

In the hearts of the blessed you'll also find iniquity. Iniquity is the wreckage of what's left of our hearts after Adam's fall. As Dorothy Sayers put it, it is the "deep interior dislocation at the very center of human personality."[14] Langdon Gilkey, reflecting on his experience in a prison camp, gets at the same point by saying that there is a "fundamental bent of the total self in all of us inward, toward our own welfare. And so immersed are we in it that we hardly are able to see this in ourselves, much less extricate ourselves from our dilemma."[15] Iniquity twists God's truth and distorts our desires. Yet the grace of being blessed is only reserved for those who have iniquity in their hearts.

Lastly, there is transgression in the heart of the blessed. This is sin in its most active and intentional energy. It sees a boundary that says "No trespassing" and walks right in. It hears someone say, "Don't cross this line," and immediately does so. It sees a speed limit sign and blows right past. It listens to God's law, a manifestation of his own character and wisdom, and says, "I don't think so. I live for my own purposes in my own power. Nobody tells me what to do!" The truth, however, still remains: the grace of God's blessing only belongs to transgressors.

---

14. Sayers, *Letters to a Diminished Church*, 59.
15. Gilkey, *Naming the Whirlwind*, 393.

A Blessed Heart

Go Ahead, Join the Club

Martin Luther once wrote a letter to his friend to encourage him because he was depressed about his struggles with sin. Luther requested that his friend "join our company and associate with us, who are real, great, and hard-boiled sinners."[16] King David is doing the same thing in Psalm 32 as he declares that he has great news for great sinners—blessedness can belong to them as they take refuge in God's grace. This grace would later be shown climactically and most fully in Christ—David's son, yet David's Lord. Luther told his friend that Jesus must be "a Savior and Redeemer from real, great, grievous and damnable transgressions and iniquities, yea, from the very greatest and most shocking sins; to be brief, from all sins added together in a grand total."[17] David isn't telling sinners to run and hide. Instead, he's telling them something different. He's telling those that see blessing as only horizontal prosperity that there is more; he's telling those who feel heart-shattering shame that there's hope. And by addressing sinners *as sinners,* David is inviting you to come and experience the extravagant grace that flows from God's heart.

God's Heart

When God's law looks at lawbreakers, it can only respond with wrath and condemnation. Pilgrim, in *The Pilgrim's Progress*, found this out when he ran into Moses, who embodies the law's strict justice in the parable. Pilgrim cried for Moses to have mercy, but he said, "I know not how to show mercy," and then he knocked Pilgrim down again, trying to kill him. However, "one came by and bid [Moses] forbear."[18] That one was Jesus.

---

16. Quoted in Brown, *Scandalous Freedom*, 69.

17. Quoted in Brown, *Scandalous Freedom*, 69. To better understand Luther's ideas on both justification and sanctification, see especially Trueman, *Luther on the Christian Life*.

18. Bunyan, *Pilgrim's Progress*, 75.

Paul argues in Romans 4 that Jesus is the fulfillment of Psalm 32.[19] The reason God can and does bless people in the "real, great, and hard-boiled sinners" club is because the Father himself, "who is rich in mercy" (Eph 2:4), gave us Christ to deal with our sin. This he does by carrying it away, covering it over, and counting us righteous.

Carried Away

God's heart is so gracious toward sinners that, in Christ, he forgives their sin. The literal meaning of the Hebrew word is to "carry away" the sin, harkening back to the scapegoat in the book of Leviticus which bears the people's sins far away into the wilderness. God himself takes all of our guilt and shame and carries it away. John Owen, the great seventeenth-century English theologian, boldly stated that bringing our sin to Jesus, by faith, "exceedingly honors him."[20] He went on to add:

> Lord, this is thy work; this is that for which thou camest into the world; this is that thou hast undertaken to do. Thou callest for my burden, which is too heavy for me to bear; take it.[21]

Even the great minds of NASA scientists have only been able to take pumpkins and launch them a mere 1.2 miles during the annual "Pumpkin Chunkin' Contest" in Pennsylvania. Jesus, though, joyfully takes all of our sin—all of it—and throws it "as far as the east is from the west" (Ps 103:12). I'd say that's pretty far and I'd say that's pretty good news. God's heart carries away our sin.

---

19. See Romans 4:6–9 in particular, but also the entire chapter for the full argument of God's justification of sinners.
20. Owen, *Works of John Owen*, 2:195.
21. Owen, *Works of John Owen*, 2:195.

A Blessed Heart

Covered Over

Not only is all our sin carried away, it is also covered over. God is so holy that he cannot look upon sin. As long as it remains exposed and uncovered, we remain separated from God. In the riches of his mercy he has provided a covering. In the Old Testament, during the day of atonement, the high priest would enter into the holy of holies with the blood of sacrifice. There he would sprinkle the mercy seat and cover it in the blood. The various sins that were evidence of a breached covenant were now covered over and mercy and blessing flowed from the tabernacle and later the temple. This was all a foreshadowing of the death of Christ, whose "precious blood" (1 Pet 1:19) covers over our futile, foolish, and fallen ways.

Whatever David had done, whatever sin or sins he had committed, had been covered over in Christ. Yours have been too. If shame fears being exposed as foolish and fallen, incapable and unlovable, grace enters the story and declares that your greatest fear has come true—everything about you has been exposed. Yet, it also declares that God, who loves you more deeply than you will ever know, has covered over your sin and shame with the blood of his own Son and desires to draw near. God's heart covers over your sin.

Counted Righteous

Even if God simply carried away our sin and covered it over, it would not yet be enough for fullness of redemption. All that would do is put us where Adam was in the garden, still needing to attain a righteousness of our own through "personal, entire, exact and perpetual obedience" to God's law.[22] God's law and our own conscience make it hard for us to believe the good news of the gospel. Our conscience reminds us that we've broken the law and agrees with the law that we should be condemned.[23] Sadly, many turn to what someone else has called living life *sola bootstrapa*—by trying

---

22. *Westminster Confession of Faith*, 19.1
23. Owen, *Works of John Owen*, 6:290–91.

to pull up our bootstraps. Forgiveness may be accepted in a shallow manner but the real issue is you getting your act together so God *really* accepts you and *really* loves you. Yet in Romans 4 Paul declares the good news that not only has our sin been imputed to Christ, but his perfect obedience and righteousness have been imputed to us. We are completely and beautifully clothed with the perfect righteousness of the One who loved us, obeyed the law on our behalf, and died bearing its curse.

The Response of a Blessed Heart

How should we respond to the gospel realities that David proclaims—that our sin is covered over, carried away, and that we are counted righteous in Christ? How should we respond when we possess and experience God's passionate and permanent favor in our lives? Two responses come to mind—repentance and worship.

First, genuine repentance—what older theologians called evangelical repentance because it is gospel-centered—is motivated by the certainty of mercy. There is a false repentance that is motivated by misery more than mercy. It is a kind of repentance which tries to self-atone with feelings of guilt to appease a fiery, judgmental, and harsh God. Rather than receiving God's grace, it is a conscious or unconscious means to earn God's favor back by trying to feel "guilty enough."[24] The heart of this repentance says, "*Maybe* God will show mercy *if* I repent enough," or "God might be merciful if I feel miserable enough." However, true repentance is motivated by the radical kindness of God expressed and promised in the gospel (Rom 2:4). It says, "God *has* shown mercy and promises that he *will* show mercy, therefore, I repent" (see 1 John 1:9). Repentance is uniquely strengthened as faith grasps the reality of justification, giving us the freedom to see our sin, confess it, and receive forgiveness for it. We'll talk more about repentance, which I'll call gospel brokenness, as we walk through the psalm together.

---

24 Calqohoun, in his masterful treatment of the subject, calls this "legal repentance." *Repentance*, 83–110.

A Blessed Heart

Second, the gravity of grace also leads to joyful worship (see especially verse 11) which is always a mark of genuine repentance.[25] When the depths, darkness, and depravity of our sin have been exposed and then dealt with by Christ at Calvary, our response is to burn with worship. We turn away from the false pleasures that sin has brought and toward the glory of God in Christ. What our hearts need most, then, is not behavior management, but worship realignment. This is how David begins this psalm. He is filled with worship because he has seen and experienced the gravity of God's grace. It's also a kind of worship that is so vibrant and genuine, coming from a heart filled with God's love, that it invites and attracts others to bathe in the light of God's love. If you're attracted to the heart that writes this psalm, keep on reading.

Moving Forward

Thankfully, God isn't like the surgeons and wizards that King Charles had. As a Divine Cardiologist he knows that healing can only take place through blessing. This blessing, though, can't come unless Christ is cursed for us and our sin is covered over, carried away, and we are counted righteous by faith. David experienced it and he wrote this psalm so that others would experience it. It's as if he is bursting at the seems to tell everyone who reads it, "God's love is deeper, wider, broader, and higher than you can ever imagine! Let me tell you about it!"

But this isn't where David started. His first step was to try to cover over his heart problems on his own. Let's just say that's a tragic choice and it's one that you and I make very often as well. In the next chapter, we'll see how that worked out for David.

Chapter Summary

While God's desire is to bless our hearts, many of us search only for "little b" blessings apart from God. Others, because of shame,

---

25. Miller, *Heart of a Servant Leader*, 202.

think they are so broken and sinful that they can never be blessed by him. Sadly, the default of our hearts is to think that God's richest blessing only belongs to those who spiritually perform. Surprisingly, God declares not the righteous, but sinners, "capital B" Blessed. They are the ones who possess and experience the deep joy of God's passionate and permanent favor in their lives. This blessing comes because God's deepest desire was to carry away our sins, cover them over, and count us righteous in Christ. In response, believers live lives of continual repentance and joyful worship.

Study Questions

1. Are there times in your life that you think God's love for you is conditioned on you getting your act together? How do you view God during these seasons?

2. If you were absolutely certain of mercy, in what areas of your life and in what specific things would you feel the freedom to repent of?

3. Will you set some time aside this week to think of specific sins in your life being carried away and covered over through the cross of Christ? What would change in your life if you really grasped that, in Christ, the Father has already declared you perfectly righteous?

3

A Transparent Heart

> Blessed is the man ... in whose spirit there is no deceit.[1]
>
> PSALM 32:2

IN THE LATE 1980S, Andre Agassi, a world-famous tennis player, was paid millions by Canon Cameras for their latest ad campaign: "Image is everything." Shortly after it began, Agassi began to hate it. People would mock him during matches and when they saw him on the street. His bad-boy image was now officially owned by corporate executives. With his famous long blond hair and cool shades, in each commercial Agassi would say "Image is everything."

And then, in his own words, catastrophe struck. In the 1990 French Open, Agassi had made his way to the final, playing someone he had already beat before and who was about to retire. In the shower the night before, Agassi used the wrong conditioner for

---

1. While other chapters spend more time on larger portions of the text, I feel this one on deceit is necessary because it is a direct application of the psalmist to the reality of God's lavish grace. Sadly, the reality of deceit mentioned in the text is largely overlooked by most commentators.

Gospel Brokenness

his hair and his hairpiece (that's right, it was a hairpiece all along because he was bald) fell apart.

> Of course I could play without my hairpiece. But after months and months of derision, criticism, mockery, I'm too self-conscious. *Image is everything?* What would they say if they knew I've been wearing a hairpiece this whole time? Win or lose, they wouldn't be talking about my game. They would only be talking about my hair. . . . the whole world would be laughing.
>
> Warming up before the match, I pray. Not for a win, but for my hairpiece to stay on. . . . My tenuous hairpiece has me catatonic. Whether or not it's slipping, I imagine it's slipping. With every lunge, every leap, I picture it landing on the clay, like a hawk my father shot from the sky. I can hear a gasp going up from the crowd. I can picture millions of people suddenly leaning closer to their TV's, turning to each other and in dozens of languages and dialects saying some version of: *Did Andre Agassi's hair* just fall off?[2]

After losing the match, Agassi talks about trying to find a place on earth where he might not feel shame. "I sit in the locker room, head bowed, imagining what the hundreds of columnists and headline writers will say. . . . I can hear them now. Image is Everything, Agassi is Nothing."[3]

In Psalm 32, David is not hiding his baldness; he may have had a mane like Fabio for all I know. But he's still hiding something which, if others find out—just like Agassi thought—will be catastrophic. At least that's more than likely what he thought initially. Agassi's questions are ones I'm fairly certain David was asking and they are questions I ask too regularly: "What would they say if they knew?" and "Where can I go to not feel this crushing shame?"

For Agassi, and for us, I believe there are two main motivators for people to wear masks—those false-fronts that are intended to present something and someone other than who we genuinely are—in order to deceive others so that we will get what we most

---

2. Agassi, *Open*, 151–53 (emphasis his).
3. Agassi, *Open*, 151–53.

deeply want. Psalm 32 simply calls this "deceit" (v. 2). It began in the garden when Adam first sewed fig leaves to try to cover himself, and has been entrenched in every fiber of our being ever since (Jer 17:9). A first reason is because we crave the attention, admiration, and affection of others. A second reason is that we are trying to cover sins, faults, and weaknesses that we don't want others to see or know about.

Creating the Mask

Being made in God's image, among many things, means that we're hardwired for relationships. We are wired to love the presence of family and friends, to enjoy their smiles, and receive their loving words of encouragement. Thus, while we are made to enjoy the attention, admiration, and affection of others, we are not to be driven by those things, nor be willing to do whatever we may need to get them. However, when we lose sight of God's gospel blessing—the deep joy of possessing and experiencing the passionate and permanent favor of God—we'll try to be whoever we need to be in order to receive the blessing of someone else's attention, admiration, or affection. Sometimes we do this knowingly, and many times we've created a mask that we're completely unaware of. As Jonathan Haidt, a moral psychologist and Professor of Ethical Leadership at New York University, has said, we're all "selfish hypocrites so skilled at putting on a show of virtue that we fool even ourselves."[4]

Known as

One reason to create a mask, driven by craving the attention, admiration, or affection of someone else, is to be known as a certain

---

4. Haidt, *Righteous Mind*, xxii. Later in his book he uses two other images to convey the same idea: first, the imagery of everyone being "intuitive politicians" who know what to do or say to get someone's vote; second, the presence within all of us of a "full-time, in-house press secretary" whose job is to justify all that we say or do, no matter how ridiculous or wrong (88, 91–92).

kind of person. As our hearts intuitively survey our relational landscapes, we've noticed that it is a certain kind of personality that draws the attention of someone by whom we want to be noticed. Generally speaking, I often tell other men that we want to make sure everyone notices the Three C's in us—we are cool, competent and in control! Perhaps it's the young teenager that notices that his parents regularly praise his older sister for her high grades but rarely say anything about his. Although he was gifted and skilled musically in ways his sister never was, he may lay those things aside about which he was most passionate and strive to become the next Einstein. Perhaps it's a newly minted college graduate heading into the workforce. Inside he is anxious and afraid, losing sleep, and forgetting to eat. Externally, if others ask how the job search is going, a calm and confident front is in place to convince others that you're just on the cusp of landing your dream job.

Frankly, and sadly, the list of masks is endless. We may pursue strength training, academic degrees, the latest fashion, or listen to the best comedians, all in an effort to be *known as* someone who is strong, smart, fashionable, or fun. Why? Because in our deepest heart we are convinced that the only way we can gain someone's attention and affection is by keeping up appearances.

Known for

Others may create a mask out of a desire to be known for doing certain things to gain the gaze of someone else. Continually doing the next dangerous thing may give you the celebrity status of being the next fully sponsored athlete for Red Bull. Constantly doing the next religious thing or always being at the church and helping out whenever—and I mean *whenever*—there is a need, may give you the ability to be known as someone who sacrifices your time for others. What is striking about this is that many of the things we exhaust ourselves doing may be good in themselves, but the reason we are doing them is to come across as a certain kind of person.

Another reason we create masks and desire to deceive is because we're trying to hide something which we don't want others to know about. Not only did Andre Aggasi want to be *known as* the bad boy of international tennis, to be *known for* his tennis skills and incredible fashion, he also desperately wanted to hide something he was ashamed of—being bald. So, the obvious means to cover that unwanted reality was having an incredible wig! He isn't the only one to struggle with this issue. Others have noted that practically all of corporate America is infected with the desire to cover over what we don't want others to see:

> In an ordinary organization, most people are doing a second job no one is paying them for. In businesses large and small; in government agencies, schools, and hospitals; in for-profits and nonprofits, and in any country in the world, most people are spending time and energy covering up their weaknesses, managing other people's impressions of them, showing themselves to their best advantage, playing politics, hiding their inadequacies, hiding their uncertainties, hiding their limitations. Hiding.[5]

Perhaps King David wanted to be known as an Israelite king who was faithful and godly, to be known for his military victories and abilities to write the latest greatest praise songs of his day. There was just one problem—he was a sinner and this psalm shows he was covering over some sin that he had committed. Like many others, David was hiding. He was covering something, deliberately deceiving others, in order to maintain appearances. Every single person reading this book does the same thing, whether in obvious or incredibly subtle ways. Whether it be sin in our lives or simple weaknesses we're ashamed of others knowing about, we do whatever it takes to cover those things over in order to retain or gain the attention, admiration, and affection of others—whether it's God or someone else's. We are all experts in image management.[6]

Return with me to your childhood when the seeds of image management are just beginning to sprout. Most children become

---

5. Kegan and Lahey, *Everyone Culture*, 1.

6. I get the language of "image management" from Scazzero, *Emotionally Healthy Leader*, 70.

resident experts in one of the oldest games of civilization—hide-and-seek. Phase I is spending time and energy, within the allotted time of the seeker who was counting with his eyes (mostly) closed, trying to find the absolute best place to hide. Phase II is about staying quietly hidden in the right place while someone is trying to find out where you really are. However, if this phase lasts too long, you begin to get annoyed. All you can hear is your own breath as you try to be quiet and hear where the finder is. Has everyone given up and started playing a new game? After too long, your heart simply says, "I wish someone would find me already. I don't much like hiding anymore."

Though mostly played during childhood, we intuitively and unconsciously play hide-and-seek throughout our lives. We hide those sinful or broken parts of us that might not be accepted by others, only allowing others to see certain things so that they won't leave us. Yet, usually over time, the heart yearns not just to be *known as* a certain kind of person or *known for* doing certain things but the heart yearns simply to *be known*.

Penetrating the Mask

Daniel Goleman, who rose to international fame after writing *Emotional Intelligence,* once said that everyone has "an almost gravitational pull toward putting out of mind unpleasant facts [about ourselves].... We tune out, we turn away, we avoid. Finally, we forget, and forget we have forgotten. A lacuna hides the harsh truth."[7] In other words, we're born deceivers, deceiving others and ourselves about how sinful we really are. A contributor to the *Huffington Post* wrote that the most effective treatment for this deep self-deception "is to be involved with people that can help keep us honest."[8] This is exactly what God does. He alone is able to help us see through our deceptions and see the ugly reality about what our hearts are actually like. He does this in three ways, each way

---

7. Goleman, *Vital Lies, Simple Truths,* 244.
8. Trosclair, "Self-Deception Is Killing Us," para. 14.

speaking increasingly clearly to our heart's true condition. He penetrates our masks through providence, through Scripture in general, and through the cross in particular.[9] Through these he reveals the masks we've created and the realities we've covered so that we'll finally put away living deceitfully and put on living honestly.

Providence Unmasks Us

First, God often uses providence to penetrate our masks. Deuteronomy 8 is the recording of God warning the Israelites of their proneness toward pride and self-sufficiency. In their forgetfulness, they might want to be *known as* a powerful nation that conquered Egypt and entered the promised land because of their own strength (Deut 8:14–19). However, part of the reason God led them through the desert was to show them what was in their hearts (Deut 8:2), and—surprise—it wasn't Egypt-conquering strength. Instead, it was God-forgetting, idol-pursuing sinfulness. God was allowing providence to shatter their self-deceptions.

Peter is another example. In his own mind, he would be strong and faithful as he stood side by side with Christ, even to the point of death. Yet once he saw Jesus being arrested and investigated, Peter ended up denying Christ three times. Rather than fighting faithfully, he would stand outside tearfully once he heard the rooster crow. Maybe he wasn't the spiritual John Wayne he thought he was.[10] Again, God used providence to shatter Peter's delusions of grandeur.

It may not be a championship tennis match, a Middle Eastern desert, or a rooster crowing that penetrates the masks of your deceptions, but various circumstances and seasons of life will come along that will begin to graciously show you that you're not as cool,

---

9. God also uses the Holy Spirit through prayer to convict us of our pretenses along with the correction or rebuke of others (see especially 2 Sam 12; Gal 2:11–14).

10. My undogmatic conviction about Peter's denial is that he denied more out of disappointment at Christ's seeming weakness as a Messiah and less from fearing death from being associated with him.

Gospel Brokenness

competent, or in control as you thought you were or wanted to appear to be for God or for others. This is a painful, but good thing.

Scripture Unmasks Us

Next, God uses his word to unmask us. Hebrews 4:12 tells us that "the word of God is living and active, sharper than any two-edged sword, piercing to the division of soul and of spirit, of joints and of marrow, and discerning the thoughts and intentions of the heart." The pride, deceit, and unbelief that lies in the secret depths of our heart is nothing compared to the "spiritual, almighty, penetrating" power of God's word.[11] If, with Augustine, we pray "Lord, show me myself!"[12] he will often do so through the sword of the word. Ironically and beautifully, as psychologist Eric Johnson states, while God's word is exceedingly sharp, its ultimate intention is to heal.[13]

The apostle Paul experienced this sword of painful healing. He created his personal mask with his inherited privileges and religious achievements (Phil 3:4–6). He was widely known as a very spiritual guy and known for his religious zeal in persecuting the church. Yet when the penetrating power of Exodus 20:17 ("You shall not covet") hit Paul, it undid him (Rom 7:7). Prior to Scripture's unmasking of his heart, Paul considered himself "blameless" as to the law (Phil 3:6), but after a lifetime of going under the scalpel of God's healing blade, he considered himself "the chief of sinners" (1 Tim 1:15). I have no doubt that if you place your heart before God's word and humbly pray, like David did in Psalm 139:23, that God would search and know your heart and then show it to you, that he will. It will be painful. It will be healing.

---

11. Owen, *Works of John Owen*, 20:359, 373.
12. Augustine, *Confessions*, 115.
13. Johnson, "One Edge of a Two-Edged Sword," 54–76.

A Transparent Heart

The Cross Unmasks Us

God uses providence and Scripture to unmask us, but most importantly, the cross does the deepest work of exposing the depths of our sin and deceit. If Isaiah was shattered by seeing God's glory in the temple (Isa 6), how much more will we tremble when we draw near to the glory displayed at Gethsemane and Calvary? For it is in Christ's deepest humiliation that his greatest glory is seen.[14] If this is true, it is also at Gethsemane and Calvary that our greatest exposure and unmasking will occur. As Fleming Rutledge comments, "The 'old Adam' in us does not want the pain of self-knowledge."[15] Yet if we want to know the depths of our deceit, to Gethsemane and Calvary we must go.

In the garden of Gethsemane, we see Jesus preparing to face the corruption that sin has caused and to endure the condemnation it deserves. He knows the next day will bring about the reality of him being made sin for us (2 Cor 5:21), enduring the curse of the law which was to be cut off, cast away, and crushed by the violent waterfall of God's justice. No wonder he was "very sorrowful, even to the point of death" (Matt 26:38). This is precisely why Christ, at Calvary, screams in unknown and unfathomable depths of agony from the cross—he didn't merely feel forsaken, he really was. That is why the Father's answer to his cry of dereliction was silence. This is why the entire sky turned black and the earth trembled in an earthquake. He was being crushed for our iniquity; he was bearing the full and horrible weight of the curse that should have fallen on you and me. Only the cross can accurately and fully expose the heinous horror that sin is and destroy its destructive deceit in our lives.

I often tell others at Christmas that the nature of the gift reveals the nature of our need. A gift someone might give may painfully expose something about us that we'd rather not face. If my twin brother sends me a tube of balding crème for Christmas,

---

14. See Reeves, *Delighting in the Trinity*, 126–27; Carson, *Gospel According to John*, 495.

15. Rutledge, *Crucifixion*, 184.

I'll have to face the reality that I'm more like Andre Agassi than I'd like to think. If my sister in Montana sends me a free membership to the gym for a year, I'll have to face the reality that the M&M's I eat every day may not have made me a world-class athlete. If my other sister in Cincinnati sent me a book entitled *5 Ways To Preach a Better Sermon*, I may have to face the fact that my preaching could drastically improve. The incarnation at Christmas and the crucifixion on Good Friday are gifts that communicate something to us if we have ears to hear—we're worse than we thought and completely unable to save ourselves. Only Christ's passion can fully penetrate our pretenses, only his degradation at Golgotha can demolish our defenses. If being with someone who can help keep us honest is the best way to dismantle our deceit, the Father has been kind in giving his Son for us, because now, as the Spirit opens our eyes to these truths, we can begin to see ourselves a little more clearly.

Taking Off the Mask

Underneath the mask at the core of our being is deep unbelief that walks through life convinced that we cannot be completely known and passionately loved. If everything about us is known, especially the masks we've worn and the things we've covered, we're convinced love won't exist for us. We may be loved, but we're also afraid of being more deeply known for fear they may run away in disgust. The cross, however, not only says that we're exhaustively known and that our darkness was finally brought to the light of Calvary, but also that we're infinitely loved. Listen to theologian J. I. Packer on the thrill of being known and loved by God:

> This is momentous knowledge. There is unspeakable comfort—the sort of comfort that energizes, be it said, not enervates—in knowing that God is constantly taking knowledge of me in love and watching over me for my good. There is tremendous relief in knowing that his love to me is utterly realistic, based at every point on prior knowledge of the worst about me, so that no discovery

now can disillusion him about me, in the way I am so often disillusioned about myself, and quench his determination to bless me.[16]

You no longer have to exhaust yourself in order to be *known as* a certain kind of person or *known for* doing certain things. You can simply delight in the beautiful reality that, by faith, you know and are known by your God. What might this mean for you?

It means you take off the mask you often wear to gain God's attention and affection. In Christ you are an adopted child and God is your Father. You'll always have his passionate attention; you'll always have his deepest affection. You don't have to cover over anything but can, with boldness, run to him in your time of need (Heb 4:16). You don't have to pray incredibly long prayers or use super religious language to pray (Matt 6:7), you simply bring your heart to him no matter what condition it is in (see the entire Psalter!). In Psalm 32, David is teaching us that he has finally learned he no longer needs to wear a Spiritual Superman cape to try to convince God he should be loved. By grace he puts away his deceit, and is honest with God.

It also means you take off the mask you wear with others. Fully accepted and lavishly loved in Christ, you are free to be who you are—someone made in God's image, possessing various gifts and skills, and also someone being remade into Christ's image who still wrestles with a multitude of sins and weaknesses. It is only the grace-empowered steady stream of repentant tears that can slowly wash away the masks we've painted over our faces so that others can know us intimately and genuinely, maybe even for the first time.

You can just imagine David grasping this and going to his roundtable for counsel—"I have sinned significantly in my life. For a season I hid it and put up a front while trying to deal with it on my own. God, though, has shown me depths of sin I was completely unaware of and showered me with superabundant mercy. Now I want to write a song about it so everyone may know." I'm

---

16. Packer, *Knowing God*, 26.

sure someone may have said, "But King David, you have an image to protect! You are—if you force me to be Captain Obvious—the king of Israel!" At an earlier point in time, David may have listened to that counsel, but in Psalm 32 he is putting away his deceit, and encouraging everyone who listens to his words to do the same.[17]

Chapter Summary

In a desire to gain the attention and affection of God or someone else, or to cover over something we don't want others to see, we often create masks of deceit. These masks enable us to be known as a certain kind of person or known for doing certain things, but they leave us not being genuinely known at all. However, in God's mercy, he penetrates our masks through his wise providence, powerful Scriptures, and Christ's glorious cross. Having experienced the grace of being fully known and yet still completely loved by God, the tears of gospel repentance wash away our masks that we've used with God and others. Now we can live in the freedom of the gospel, being humbly honest about our strengths, sins, and weaknesses.

Study Questions

1. When you lose sight of the gospel, who do you want to be known as or what do you want to be known for? What kind of image do you want to put up for others to see? Why?

2. Has there been an experience in your life—whether through providence, Scripture, prayer, or an interaction with someone else—where God in his grace unmasked you?

---

17. It may be important to mention at this point what I don't mean by transparency. I do not mean the ability to be overly open in such a way that you're simply drawing attention to yourself or that you're exaggerating some of your brokenness to impress people with how much you get the gospel. I simply mean not putting up a mask and being open to the extent it is helpful in serving others in their Christian walks.

3. Many scholars believe that Peter is the eyewitness behind Mark's account of the gospel. Incredibly, the account of Peter's denial is the longest and most detailed in Mark's account of Christ's passion. Why do you think this is? How does this encourage you and apply to you?

4. Secure in Christ's sin-forgiving, shame-covering love, who are you when the masks come off?

4

An Exhausted Heart

> For when I kept silent, my bones wasted away through my groaning all day long. For day and night your hand was heavy upon me; my strength was dried up as by the heat of summer. Selah
>
> PSALM 32:3-4

IN THE 1920S, THE Hooker Chemical Company purchased the Love Canal, which was close to Niagara Falls. It was dug out to produce electricity, but the previous owner lost funding before the project could be finished. It was, in the minds of the chemical company's leadership, an ideal place to pour their chemical waste. In the 1950s, the company covered over the old canal—along with millions of gallons of waste contained in metal barrels—with only a few feet of dirt. To make sure they fulfilled their civic duties, they even sold the property to the city for the deal of the century: $1.

The city went on to build neighborhoods and even a school on the property. Eventually, however, "black goo" (an actual term used by the scientists of the time) began to bubble up from the ground. The city, realizing it had made a mistake, continued to tell the community that it wasn't a big problem and that they

An Exhausted Heart

should continue their lives as usual. Yet continuing your life as usual remains hard when you mysteriously become ill, some of your friends require surgery, and others are overcome by serious respiratory issues. Cases of cancer and birth defects began to pop up everywhere, but the chemical company and the city continued to reassure people that the problem was manageable.

The depths of the issue could no longer stay hidden when, in 1977, a blizzard saturated the ground enough for more chemicals to begin leaking out of the ground. Corroded chemical barrels that had been buried were falling apart and spewing their corruption everywhere. In-ground pools slowly started rising above the ground, floating on ponds of chemicals. Schools shut down as chemicals leaked into hallways. Eventually, scientists identified over 400 harmful chemicals, some deadly, leaking from the ground. Most families were relocated out of town by the government, only after action by the community members.[1]

When we try to cover over or deal with sin in our own strength and with our own strategies, it won't only take a massive toll on us personally, but eventually the truth will leak out and we'll have to face the relational toll our failure to confess our sins takes on others. David experienced this and now he's sharing his story with us.

Because David has grasped the magnitude of grace, he is giving us the profound privilege of looking at his Spirit-inspired heart scans—not only that we will know his heart, but so that we will know ours as well. His gospel transparency will enable us to see the wrong assumptions he made, the tragic strategies he implemented to try to deal with sin on his own, and the consequences that covering his corruption had on himself and others.

---

1. Beck, "Love Canal Tragedy."

Gospel Brokenness

Wrong Assumptions Made

Like David, our struggles with sin are often founded on enormously wrong assumptions about the power of sin, our ability to fight it, and what God is like in the midst of our struggles.

Sin: Minimal and Manageable

One aspect of sin's ability to overcome us is its deceitfulness (see Heb 3:13). It is highly trained in camouflaging what it actually is. This is seen in how we often think that sin—whether it be deeply distorted desires, ways of thinking about ourselves or others, or ways of relating to others—will create no big problems. Like the leaders at the chemical company, sin wants to convince us that it really is a minimal problem that will do little to harm us, others, and our relationship with God. So, our hearts engage sin and consider it more like harmlessly indulging in a little dessert and less like intentionally ingesting massive amounts of rat poison. When we view sin as a minor problem, we've been massively deceived and we'll remain silent.

It not only camouflages the problems it creates, but also the power it possesses. Floyd Mayweather Jr. is only 5 feet 8 inches tall and weighs under 150 pounds. He's not a big guy by any stretch of the imagination. Some people might only know him from his quite terrible dance debut on *Dancing with the Stars* in 2007 where he was quickly eliminated. If you saw him in his dance clothes, you might think, "I could take that guy, easy." However, it might literally hit you once you saw him in boxing shorts that he's one of the most powerful, successful boxers to ever step foot in the ring and who really likes knocking guys out. Sin will wear nice clothes and invite you to dance, but it won't show you its power right away. As long as the dance continues, you still think it's not that powerful and therefore fairly manageable. When we view sin as manageable, we've been massively deceived and we'll remain silent.

An Exhausted Heart

Self: Capable

Not only does sin cause us to underestimate its power, it also causes us to overestimate ours. This may look like the inwardly confident, "I got this, I can handle it," or the more nervous, "I have to find a way to fix this and make it right." Either way, it is self-reliance at its core. If sin is minor and manageable and I am capable, then I can stop when I need to and change whenever and however I want. You might as well call me Superman.

This was the problem with the Hooker Chemical Company. In their minds, the chemicals in the canal weren't really a major problem. In fact, just a few feet of dirt could easily cover everything over. Problem solved. And for David? When you look in verse 4 when he says, "I didn't cover over my sin," he is implying that up to that point he thought he could deal with it in his own strength and cover it over. He remained silent because he didn't need to confess. Whatever the issue was, he could deal with it on his own.

With these things in mind—sin as minor and manageable and self as capable—we usually respond in one of three general non-gospel ways.[2] We can continue in rebellion, enjoying "the pleasures of sin" (Heb 11:25) and convince ourselves that we'll give it up if necessary whenever we need to. We might use religion as our covering, convincing ourselves that making more promises to do better and multiplying religious rituals will help us deal with this minor and manageable nuisance in our lives. And finally, rather than outright rebellion or commitment to religion, we respond with simple indifference. If you could see inside, we have the "meh" emoji tattooed on the DNA of every cell inside us. "Seriously, what's the big deal? And did you see Mark's new big-screen TV? It's amazing."

Seeing ourselves as being capable in the fight against sin or the need to cover it over will keep us silent, unwilling to confess it.

---

2. More specific ways will be outlined below.

God: Vengeful

Wrong assumptions about what God's heart is like or how he will respond to our sin also keep us from confessing. Satan and sin want to convince us that God is "*only* an Avenger and Judge" and therefore the thought of confessing to him or running toward him "overwhelms us" and we stay away.[3] God is and will be exceedingly harsh with us so it's better to not even get close.[4] If we consider God as a cosmic Mike Tyson, who was willing, eager, and ready to bite off a chunk of our ear if we messed up and then had the audacity to come close to him, it seems more than reasonable that we'll remain distant and silent, especially if you like the way your ears look.

Seeing God as any less merciful than he actually is will only drive us into our own resources and into relying on our own strategies to deal with sin. This, too, will keep us silent.

Tragic Strategies Implemented

We may or may not be consciously aware that our heart is making the above assumptions. Yet we move forward by trying to deal with the sin of which we're aware. Various strategies in dealing with ourselves, God, and others are implemented so that we don't have to experience being humbled and seeing our desperate need for forgiveness and cleansing.

Strategies for Ourselves

First, we have habitual strategies to deal with sin. Three that seem to be most prominent are minimizing, rationalizing, and comparing. When we minimize sin, we convince ourselves that whatever sin we're allured by isn't that big of a deal, and besides, it's not hurting anyone. In fact, it may be such a small matter to us we have

---

3. Calvin, *Institutes*, 3.3.4; (emphasis mine).
4. Owen, *Works of John Owen*, 2:34.

grown to not even give it a second thought. Another option is to rationalize our sin. We can point to circumstances that are incredibly difficult, like a terrible job, a lazy spouse, kids that are out of control, classes that aren't going well, a breakup, etc. Anything can be an excuse to simply indulge in a little sin periodically. Or, if one is a little more honest, whatever sin it may be, it just gives you a little bit of joy, rest, and satisfaction. Last, comparing ourselves to others is another strategy our deceitful hearts can engage in. At least we don't get as angry at our kids as our friends do. I'm not addicted to pornography like those guys in that church recovery group, I just look every few days. And, have you seen how often Jenny posts on Instagram? She can be so judgmental. I just post cat videos all day. Minimizing, rationalizing, and comparing will keep us viewing sin as manageable, ourselves as capable, and leave us silent in our relationship with God.

Strategies for God

Next, we have habitual strategies in our dealing with God that help us justify our sin. A major strategy that has been in our bloodline ever since the fall of Adam has been to blame God. Sometimes, this reality is so deep that we're completely unaware that this is what we are doing. Over time and with life's little and big disappointments and struggles, we come to believe that God hasn't given us the life we wanted so we'll try to create that life for ourselves and make it happen. In the end, however, it really is all God's fault. A little reflection will show how large a portion of our sin is driven by a deeply rooted anger that God hasn't been good to us.

The nature of sin, though, is also to deceive and harden. Whether initially, or eventually, sin convinces us to simply ignore what God says. He ruins all of my fun and hasn't done anything for me anyway. Why should I want to do what he tells me to do?

Strategies for Others

One of the greatest myths of our day, in my opinion, is that if what we do in private doesn't hurt anyone, it's not wrong. Yet this completely misunderstands the nature of sin and its ability to harden the heart. When our hearts are hardened, we bear less fruit from the Spirit, which in turn leads to massive impacts on how we relate to others. One way sin can affect us is to make us cynical. It makes things in creation seem to be majestic whereas it minimizes the majesty of God. When God holds no weight in our lives he's literally of no consequence to us. When we sense that we've experienced little to no change, we don't really expect others to change either. Cynicism is uniquely insightful into how profoundly broken everything is, but also deeply blind as to the power of redemption.

Sin will also make you critical. It is the nature of sin to blind you to your own corruption while giving you 20/20 vision for the faults and failures of others. This especially is how David's heart expressed how he covered his sin. We see this in 2 Samuel 12, when David has committed adultery and murder and yet nobody knows about it (or so he thinks). The prophet Nathan comes to him with a parable about a rich man who steals the cherished lamb of a poor family in order to entertain and feed a visiting friend. Fuming and enraged, David declares that the rich man "deserves to die" (2 Sam 12:5). David saw more condemnable sin in someone who simply stole a lamb when he had stolen a man's wife and killed her husband in the process. When we remain unbroken for our sin, we will break others with our selfish frustration and quick criticism.

The Consequences of Covering Our Corruption

Just as it should've been obvious that there would be enormous consequences for simply covering over toxic waste with a few feet of dirt, so Scripture is very clear that we will experience tremendous consequences when sin remains unconfessed and we remain

An Exhausted Heart

unrepentant.[5] As one scholar says, "so long as the tongue refused to speak the words of repentance, it curled in speechless pain."[6] These painful consequences will be personal and relational.

Personal Consequences

A personal consequence mentioned in this psalm is the total loss of strength—his bones wasted away and his "strength was dried up as in the heat of summer" (v. 3). Not only has sin taken away physical strength from David, but it also primarily has taken away spiritual strength from him. Sin makes pursuing God in any way—reading Scripture, prayer, attending worship, meditation—seem like an intolerable or almost impossible burden. It even weakens our *desire* to do these things. Let this psalm warn all those who read it—sin will take away spiritual vitality.

Not only does it strip us of spiritual strength, but it can lead to heart-splitting sorrow. We'll deal more with this when we navigate verse 10 in a later chapter, but there are many sorrows that will come upon those who seek to live in sin and try to cover it up. Let me mention a couple here—it takes away our assurance of God's love and it weakens our communion with him. When we turn toward sin, we're turning away from the loving face of our Father, the gracious heart of our Savior, and the comforting presence of the Spirit. Not only do we lose communion with the One who is Life itself, but we lose the deep assurance of his inexhaustible love for even his wayward children. Eventually, one cannot at least feel a hint of this sorrow overtaking the heart that has drifted away from God.

Relational Consequences

Relationally, sin makes us shallow and isolated. If we're working hard to cover things up, no one will genuinely know who we are.

---

5. See especially Psalm 6:2–3; 38:2–10; 51:8; 102:3–7; 143:4.
6. Craigie and Tate, *Psalms 1–50*, 267.

There are few, if any, that *really* know what's going on inside of you because you are covering things over and protecting your image. Sin also isolates us as it gradually convinces the heart to live more for ourselves than others (2 Cor 5:15; Phil 2:21). Living in unrepentant sin is like living in a house without ever taking the garbage out. People may come over at first, but eventually no one will want to get close.

God Strategically Enters the Silence

He Shatters Our Assumptions

As things get beyond your ability to control, your initial assumptions may need to be revised or completely rejected. When you finally get the picture that a few feet of dirt won't contain chemicals or keep others from getting terminally ill, you don't throw a few more feet of dirt on top and hope for the best. You shut down your company and ask the EPA to spend billions of tax-payer dollars to clean up your mess. When you finally realize the delicious dessert you were enjoying had rat poison in it, you don't nicely ask the waiter for the check, take a sip of wine, and head out to see your 8 o'clock movie. You scream for help and tell someone to call 911. When the person you were having fun with at the dance party isn't simply some small guy you could easily beat, but a world-class boxer mercilessly beating you senseless, you don't try to win him over by telling a Chuck Norris joke. You want someone stronger—like Chuck Norris—to make him stop so you have enough time to run to safety. In each situation, the problems that once seemed minor and manageable—with yourself as the capable hero—become the overwhelming reality that you can't save yourself and fix what has happened on your own. You finally realize you are not Superman and you desperately need help.

God, in his incomprehensible wisdom and immeasurable grace, shatters our previous assumptions about sin, ourselves, and God.[7] The sin that we have in our hearts doesn't create minor

---

7. Note Psalm 51:6 ("you teach me truth in my inward being").

problems but incredible, awful, complex, and sometimes long-lasting problems, not only for us, but also for those we are closest to. Indulging any sin for any amount of time isn't simply indulging in a little dessert, but ingesting rat poison, and you need someone else to rescue you from its deadly effects. Nor is sin manageable because it's not really powerful. It's murderously powerful and eager for the kill. Once we are entangled in its grip, we need a Champion who will fight for us and deal a death blow to it. And God, driven by a deep love that far exceeds our ability to understand, is excited and eager to be that Champion for you.

He Disrupts Our Strategies

First Samuel 5 is one of the only other places where the language of a hand being "heavy against" someone is used. The Philistines had conquered Israel in battle and they wanted to show their own people and all Israel how strong their god—Dagon—was by placing the ark inside Dagon's temple. However, God's "heavy hand" afflicted them with various sicknesses, disrupting their strategy to show the world their superiority (1 Samuel 5:6, 11). This shows, then, that God's heavy hand is used to disrupt sinners from living for their own purposes and in their own power.

This heavy hand was graciously laid upon David in order to disrupt his self-reliant strategy to deal with sin on his own. Though he could very well have experienced terrible physical weaknesses and sickness, he is more than likely describing how he was feeling spiritually. He was shaken to his very core ("my bones wasted away"[8]) and he was confronted with his absolute, total weakness to deal with sin on his own ("my strength was dried up"[9]).[10] God does this not because he is "only an Avenger and a Judge" but because he is a loving Father with a heart filled with grace deeper than Mt.

---

8. Ps 32:3.

9. Ps. 32:3.

10. Calvin states that the Spirit often allows sin to remain in believers in order "to humble them by the consciousness of their own weakness" (*Institutes*, 3.3.11).

Gospel Brokenness

Everest is tall (see Heb 12:7–10). We are his children that he cannot allow to finally and fully walk away from the Source of life. Yet just as each of us are different people with different struggles with sin, God knows how to wisely and perfectly deal with each of us:

> God deals with his saints in great variety; some shall have all their bones broken, when others shall have only the gentle strokes of the rod. *We are in the hand of mercy,* and he may deal with us as seems good unto him . . ."[11]

The sharp pain we may feel is not the hatchet of a butcher, but the precise incision of the best Surgeon. The agony we may experience isn't the crushing blow from an unexpected street assault, but a wise physical therapist who knows when to push the discomfort button up—not to restrict freedom, but to restore and expand it. "His rescue may hurt us, but the goal is always our safety and the motive is always his love."[12]

One cannot help but feel the impression that as David wrote this section of the psalm, his heart grieved with sorrow. He was reminded not only of the sin he had committed, but also the strategies he employed to cover it up and the strength he expended in the process. That's one of the core aspects of genuine gospel brokenness—sorrowing over sin. We sorrow not only over the guilt that sin brings, but also the corrosion and corruption it unleashes in our soul. We sorrow not only over our strategies to deal with it on our own, but that sin had taken us into "the far country" (Luke 15:13) away from the heart of our Father.

---

11. Owen, *Works of John Owen*, 6:350 (emphasis mine). Also Calvin, *Institutes* 3.8.5: ". . . the Lord himself, according as he sees it expedient, confronts us and subjects and restrains our unrestrained flesh with the remedy of the cross. And this he does in various ways in accordance with what is healthful for each man. For not all of us suffer in equal degree from the same diseases or, on that account, need the same harsh cure. From this it is to be seen that some are tried by one kind of cross, others by another. But since the heavenly physician treats some more gently but cleanses others by harsher remedies, while he wills to provide for the health of all, yet he leaves no one free and untouched, because he knows that all, to a man, are diseased."

12. Chapell, *Holiness by Grace*, 180.

Yet so that we can always trust the Father no matter what might come our way, the same hands that pressed against David in Psalm 32 are the hands of the Son that will be pierced for David at Calvary. The hands that press against you and me whenever we sin and pursue self-reliant strategies are not the hands of a fighter coming to get his pound of flesh, but the hands of a Savior who gave his flesh for us on the cross. As David was silent when he struggled to cover over his sin, the Savior was silent as he went to the slaughter of Golgatha in order to cover over David's sin—and ours (Isa 53:7; Acts 8:32).

Chapter Summary

When we try to cover over sin on our own, we make disastrous assumptions. We assume that sin is minor and manageable, that we are capable, and that God is vengeful. These assumptions lead to tragic strategies: for ourselves, we minimize and rationalize sin or compare our sin to others; we either blame God for our struggles or completely ignore him; and we become cynical or critical toward others. Yet there are consequences of covering our corruption. Personally, we lose spiritual strength and multiply our sorrows; relationally we can become isolated and shallow. God, in his grace, strategically enters our silence, shattering our assumptions. He shows us that we are not strong, that sin is not manageable, and that he is extravagantly gracious. He also, with the loving discipline of a father, frustrates our strategies with his heavy hand. It is this same Father who gave his Son to die, so that his blood—rather than our foolish strategies—would cover our sin.

Study Questions

1. What are ways that you try to justify sin to yourself?
2. Do you have strategies that you use to cover over sin rather than confess it?

Gospel Brokenness

3. In what specific ways does sin disrupt your relationship with God and others in your life?

4. Has God's heavy but gracious hand ever led you to confess known sin? Mention a time you experienced this.

5. What ways of viewing God will keep you from him? Draw you toward him?

5

A Confessing Heart

> I acknowledged my sin to you, and I did not cover my iniquity; I said, "I will confess my transgressions to the LORD," and you forgave the iniquity of my sin. Selah
>
> PSALM 32:5

OPENLY ACKNOWLEDGING WEAKNESS OR clearly confessing that you have done something wrong seems to be inviting certain rejection and condemnation. This is dramatically seen in Victor Hugo's famous work, *The Hunchback of Notre Dame*. It seems like the entire story is characterized by one word: rejection. Early in the story, our hearts break as the newly born Quasimodo is rejected by his own mother because of his hideous deformities. The local church places him on a table in a public square in the hopes someone might adopt him, but it ends up being a sideshow of humiliation. One woman even states out loud, "I truly hope . . . that nobody will offer to take him."[1] Rejected by his mother. Rejected by all the passersby. Rejected.

---

1. Hugo, *Hunchback of Notre Dame*, 123.

Another character in the story is the beautiful Esmerelda. Through an unfortunate turn of events, she is wrongly arrested and tortured for the death of a man named Phoebus, a local Captain America lookalike that all the girls swoon over. Phoebus is not really dead (though no one knows this) nor did Esmerelda have anything to do with the attack on him. Yet she is tortured so painfully that she falsely confesses to murdering Phoebus just to end the agony.

The judge, who was watching the torture says, "In confessing, you have only to look for death."[2]

Not only classic literature but our own experience seems to convince our conscience and persuade our hearts that confession should never be an option because it practically guarantees rejection and condemnation. Yet the message of the gospel and the power of the Spirit shouts with a megaphone even louder than the clamoring of our guilty hearts and convinces us of the kindness of God. It is the certainty of mercy and the Spirit convincing us of God's kindness that leads us to take the first step onto the pathway of repentance.

The Foundation of Gospel Brokenness

Motivation—what drives us to do what we do—is crucial to understand gospel brokenness. In 2 Corinthians 7:10, Paul warns against a kind of repentance that actually leads to death. This repentance sees the danger of sin and feels the gravity of its guilt, but fearing God's anger, it turns in self-reliance to try to make amends either through trying to feel miserable enough or trying to do enough good to appease a deeply angry Judge. Self-reliant fear, with a drive to fix things on your own, Paul says, will land you at the doorstep of spiritual death.

In contrast, godly repentance—what we're calling gospel brokenness—is driven by an entirely different motivation: "What gives repentance power is not the *guilt* evoked by the Law alone

---

2. Hugo, *Hunchback of Notre Dame*, 266.

(Rom 7:7), but the *grace* proclaimed to us only in the gospel of our Lord Jesus Christ. It is the kindness of God that leads to repentance" (Rom 2:4).[3]

One way God expresses his kindness toward us is his actually giving repentance to us as a blood-bought gift of the Son (Acts 5:31; 11:18; 2 Tim 2:25). This gift of gospel brokenness, sovereignly and lovingly given by the Father, through the Son, and in the power of the Spirit, opens the eyes of our heart to see and sense clearly and deeply both the character of sin and the character of God.

The Character of Sin

Gospel brokenness understands that the spiritual deformity that sin causes within our hearts is incredibly more appalling than the physical deformity that the Hunchback of Notre Dame had to sadly endure. Jesus, the perfect Knower of the heart, taught that sin isn't simply something we do; rather, it's the crippled condition of our hearts:

> For from within, out of the heart of man, come evil thoughts, sexual immorality, theft, murder, adultery, coveting, wickedness, deceit, sensuality, envy, slander, pride, foolishness. All these evil things come from within, and they defile a person. (Mark 7:21–23)

The actions of sin that we might experience or see in our own lives have their source deep within the subterranean caverns of our disordered hearts. The *Westminster Confession of Faith* calls this "original corruption."[4] This phrase, "original corruption," is seeking to communicate that every aspect of our being—our ability to think, feel, choose, desire—is infected with the disease of sin and corrupts our every thought, word, and deed. Yes, the gospel gives us a new heart for which we will be eternally thankful, but the remnants of this original corruption will always remain an unwelcome guest until we arrive safely in glory.

---

3. Ferguson, *Grace of Repentance*, 53 (emphasis his).
4. See ch. 6, sec. 4.

If we only focus on the outward aspects of sin, we'll fail because we think dealing with sin is manageable. All we have to do is simply choose to do something different and clean up our act. It's like someone who has a leak in their roof and they simply clean up after every rain rather than going to the source and fixing the roof. Yet most people don't know anything about fixing a roof and nobody can fix the diseased and corrupt condition of our hearts.

Except God.

Which is why David is finally and fully confessing his sin and why he is encouraging us to do the same. He is finally feeling and acknowledging the reality that sin has become so intertwined with every cell of his being that he doesn't have the wisdom or strength to know how to untangle himself from its innumerable tentacles. Knowing God's kindness, gospel brokenness cries for help to overcome the corrupt condition from which all sin springs because we have finally been convinced that we can't fix the problem.

Original corruption, however, isn't only a condition from which sin springs, but also a disposition toward which sin directs. This is what the word "iniquity" strives to communicate as sin is a kind of bentness that seeks to drive us away from God. Sin, then, not only points us in the wrong direction, away from the Source of Life, but also has the power to drive us back into the desert. Thus, in general, sin's disposition is to point us away from God, but more particularly it seeks to convince us, whether we know it or not, to live in our own power for our own selfish purposes.

Remember as we saw in Psalm 32:4, when David strove to do life in his own power, it made him exhausted. While being made in God's image means that a core aspect of our humanity is that we are dependent on our Creator for *everything*, the disposition of our heart is to rely on our own strength. After all, isn't life about growing up and becoming independent? Well, yes, when it comes to the common life of going to school, getting a job or learning a trade, and seeking to provide for yourself and those dependent on you. Living this way spiritually, however, is a disaster. It leads us to either confidently say, "I've got this," or fearfully say, "I have to make this work!" This is why, in contrast, Paul says, "be strong *in the Lord* and in *the strength of his might*."[5]

Our disposition isn't only to live in our own power, but to live for our own purposes. Prior to his incarceration in a Japanese internment camp, Langdon Gilkey was an atheist who confidently proclaimed the goodness of all humanity. However, his experience among fellow prisoners painfully taught him that there was a "fundamental bent of the total self in all of us inward, toward our own welfare. And so immersed are we in it that we hardly are able to see this in ourselves, much less extricate ourselves from our dilemma."[6] This is why Paul states that only the gospel can empower us to "no longer live for ourselves" (2 Cor 5:5). In addition, not only do we live for ourselves, but each of us—because of our culture, family, life experiences, education, passions, etc.—pursues living for ourselves in ways unique to our own hearts.

With the eyes of his heart opened by the kindness of God, David realizes that the riptide of sin's disposition has taken him far from God. So far, in fact, that he cannot swim back. In gospel brokenness, he cries out in confession that he needs God's rescuing grace.

Rooted in a condition of original corruption, fueled by a selfish disposition, sinful actions eventually come to fruition. Whether it's a thought, word, or deed, it reeks of darkness and selfishness. What are the consequences? It leaves us guilty, shamed, and condemned, corrupting our character and hardening our hearts. Gospel brokenness, by the grace of God, sees with increasing accuracy the twisted character of sin. Though it's hard to look at, it's evidence of the kindness of God at work in our lives.

The Character of God

The gift of gospel brokenness helps us see with increasing clarity the nature of sin not only by looking directly at sin, but by having

---

5. Eph 6:10; emphasis mine.
6. Gilkey, *Shantung Compound*, 115.

the eyes of our hearts opened to the character of God. Gospel brokenness gradually grows through realizing that God is holier and more righteous than we thought and more merciful than we could ever imagine.

First, God is holier and more righteous than we thought. Sin loves to darken and diminish the brightness and greatness of God's holiness in our eyes. This is why Jesus says that our sinful hearts naturally hate the light because it will expose our darkness (John 3:20). God, with an even greater and more passionate love for us, will allow our hearts to see and experience his blinding holiness that we might see sin more clearly. One of Scripture's clearest examples of this is the experience of the prophet Isaiah (Isa 6). Prior to encountering God, he was an upstanding citizen of Israel and worshiper of his God. Yet when God actually showed up and drew near to Isaiah, he was shattered and undone (Isa 6:5) because he realized he was far more sinful than he had previously thought.

It's important, at this juncture, to make a crucial point. There are words that describe God's character in Scripture that are absolutely true; yet, if we place the word *only* in front of those words, they become deceptively false. For instance, God is a Judge—true. One day he will restore justice and make everything right again. But to say that God is *only* a Judge is patently false and would do nothing but strike fear into our hearts and keep us away from him. God is love—wonderfully true. But to say that God is *only* love is deceptively false and would lead us to view him as a cosmic Barney the dinosaur, someone we could easily dismiss. Thus, God is holier and more righteous than we thought and therefore we see sin more clearly, but he is not *only* holy and righteous.

He is, second, more merciful and gracious than we could ever imagine. In one of his well-known short stories, "The Capital of the World," Ernest Hemingway tells about a father who was looking for his son:

> Madrid is full of boys named Paco, which is the diminutive of the name Francisco, and there is a Madrid joke about a father who came to Madrid and inserted an advertisement in the personal columns of *El Liberal* which

said: Paco meet me at Hotal Montana noon Tuesday all is forgiven Papa, and how a squadron of Guardia Civil had to be called out to disperse the eight hundred young men who answered the advertisement.[7]

While the story is referring to a joke in Madrid about the enormous number of boys named Paco, it is ultimately about something vastly more important—an abiding sense that we need to be forgiven, and that there is a father who is willing to and longs to forgive. This is precisely what David experienced and is telling us in this psalm.

One of the core descriptions of God's character in Scripture is found in Exodus 34. The Lord passes before Moses and preaches a mini-sermon to him:

> The LORD passed before him and proclaimed, "The LORD, the LORD, a God merciful and gracious, slow to anger, and abounding in steadfast love and faithfulness."
> (34:6)

As a king of Israel, David would have a copy of God's law, which included the books of Moses, which included the words just quoted above (Deut 17:18–19). Perhaps it was these verses from Exodus that David read and realized that God's holiness not only brings a deeper conviction for sin, but in his mercy, he has promised to forgive our sin.

It is understanding the riches of grace, the extravagance of mercy, and the fullness of forgiveness that drives us to gospel repentance, especially after Calvary, where God's holiness and mercy kissed each other.[8] The harsh judge of *The Hunchback of Notre Dame* told Esmerelda, "In confessing you have only to look for death,"[9] but in the grace of God we can confess our sin and hear the staggering words, "all is forgiven." Not "all *might* be forgiven," or "*some* is forgiven," but "all is forgiven." These words invite sinners

---

7. Hemingway, *Complete Short Stories of Ernest Hemingway*, 29.
8. See Psalm 85:10.
9. Hugo, *Hunchback of Notre Dame*, 266.

like us to come home to the embrace of our Father. Listen to these words from John Owen:

> God forgives in a rejoicing, triumphant manner . . . satisfying abundantly his own holy soul therein. . . . We think it our duty to pray, to hear the word, to give alms, to love the brethren, and to abstain from sin; and if we fail in any of these, we find the guilt of them reflected upon our conscience, unto our disquietment: *but we scarce think it our duty to believe the forgiveness of sins.*[10]

Do these words stir your heart to turn from sin and turn back to the heart of God?

The Expression of Gospel Brokenness

God is teaching us, through David, that we don't need to hide our sin or deal with it on our own. When we know that God forgives in "a rejoicing, triumphant manner,"[11] we know we have the freedom to confess our sin to him with the anticipation of being forgiven and cleansed.[12] It is in light of God's forgiving grace that David's confession of gospel brokenness is comprehensive, personal, and relational.

Gospel Brokenness is Comprehensive

Notice, first, that his confession in this verse is comprehensive. In one verse, David uses the language of rebellion five times: sin (two times), iniquity (two times), and transgressions (one time). David is realizing and confessing that in every act or season of rebellion against our God or sin against others, there is a host of things going on inside his heart. Instead of aiming for the glory of God, he has been aiming for his own purposes, thus falling short (sin) of God's. Instead of staying within the boundary lines of God's kingdom,

---

10. Owen, *Works of John Owen*, 6:504 (emphasis mine).
11. Owen, *Works of John Owen*, 6:504.
12. See 1 John 1:9.

he creates his own boundaries as he builds his self-oriented kingdom (transgression). Rather than move toward the well of living waters flowing from God's heart, his heart has bent away, looking for water in dirty cisterns somewhere else (iniquity; Jer 2:13). In all this, he is seeking to comprehensively confess the condition, disposition, and actions of his heart to his God.

An initial step in our confession, then, as we learn from David, is a confession that is free and full. By free I mean that it is not forced or coerced; instead, it comes freely from the heart because we've been convinced that we cannot deal with the depth, corruption, and guilt of sin on our own. It's also full because we are not hiding anything, but want to bring everything in our heart to the light, so that it can be seen, confessed, and forgiven in order that our hearts can be cleansed and transformed.[13]

Gospel Brokenness is Personal

His confession is also personal—"*my* sin," "*my* iniquity," "*my* transgressions," "the iniquity of *my* sins" (Ps 32:5). In confession, David is laying down some of the most strategic weapons that sin often uses—deceitfulness, blaming other people, blaming circumstances, and outright excusing. He completely, honestly, and personally acknowledges his sin as his own. In doing this, he is acknowledging "I am guilty, I deserve justice. I cry for mercy. I have done these things; they have come from my heart. There is no one else to blame."

As we sit next to David in the school of gospel brokenness, we should, like him, seek to make our confession deeply personal by laying down our usual weapons of strategically blaming circumstances or people. We can acknowledge our sin with the certainty of mercy as our greatest motivator.

---

13. For more on the freeness and fullness of confession, see Owen, *Works of John Owen*, 6:372.

Gospel Brokenness is Relational

Last, David's confession isn't simply comprehensive and personal, but also relational. His sin wasn't simply falling short of some impersonal goal, but a falling short of his Creator's design and his heavenly Father's desire. His transgression wasn't simply the crossing of an impersonal boundary, but the crossing of his King's will; his iniquity wasn't simply an inner bentness, but an inner bentness away from the One who created and redeemed him. That is why David says, "I acknowledged my sin *to you* . . . I will confess my transgressions *to the LORD*" (Ps 32:5).

When we confess our sin, we are confessing to the Father, Son, and Spirit our need for extravagant grace and exhaustive forgiveness. We have left the Father's home, treated the Son and his work at Calvary with indifference, and grieved the heart of the Spirit. Confession must treat God not only as up there on his throne, but also as in our heart, near, able to hear our confession and interact with us personally.

While David's confession in this verse and our categories of confession as comprehensive, personal, and relational are instructive, we cannot treat them as a rigid list of what repentance must look like every time. It is not the quality, depth, or length of our repentance that grants us forgiveness, but the beautiful reality of grace that's always greater than our sin. Sometimes, it's sufficient simply to say, "God, be merciful to me, a sinner" (Luke 18:13).

The Experience of Forgiveness

Is confession, then, as we stated at the beginning of the chapter, inviting certain rejection and condemnation? Does David have to wait a few hours, days, or weeks as God deliberates on if he wants to forgive this wayward earthly king or not? This verse, I believe, shows that grace catches sinners off guard with hair-trigger mercy.

A Confessing Heart

Caught Off Guard

There are three things that keep us from experiencing God's forgiveness. First, our conscience condemns us (Rom 2:15; 1 John 3:20). It's like a policeman reminding us that we have broken the law and we have the right to remain silent and pay our dues in jail. It does not have the authority nor power to pronounce any kind of forgiveness, thus, we don't expect it. Second, God's law condemns us (Gal 3:10; Jas 2:10). The law, apart from God's saving grace, can only criticize and condemn. Its constant message is, "That wasn't good enough," "You shouldn't have done that," "You deserve punishment." The law, then, joins with our conscience to lead us to fear God and not to expect mercy. Last, our fallen views of God, which we've mentioned already, hinder us from expecting forgiveness. Our hearts often view God as *only* a Judge who is eager and willing to condemn.[14] Like Esmerelda, in confessing we expect condemnation.

Or maybe not.

Maybe we expect some form of penance. I think we often default to two kinds of penance. One form is misery. If we just try to make ourselves miserable enough for long enough, then maybe our misery can make us clean and we can come back to God. Or, on the other hand, there is the penance of the marathon race. We might expect God to say, "I heard you confess your sin. That's well and good. So, start running. If you can do ten laps around Mt. Sinai, I'll consider having mercy." Or, more realistically, maybe we think it's a marathon of new obedience—maybe Scripture reading every day, ten hours of prayer, volunteering at the homeless shelter every week, never saying a harsh word to my kids again, or whatever. We can turn practically anything into a kind of spiritual penance.[15] The last thing we would expect is forgiveness from God

---

14. These three hindrances to experiencing forgiveness come from Owen, *Works of John Owen*, 6:386–91.

15. To be abundantly clear, "new obedience" is extremely important in the Christian life, as God, in Spirit-wrought sanctification, makes us more like Jesus. The difference, however, is that our devotion is not done in order to be forgiven, but because we are forgiven. *Forgiveness is the fuel that drives the fire*

that is immediate, full, and free. Yet this is exactly what God gives to repentant sinners which is precisely why it catches us off guard every time.

Hair-Trigger Mercy

Scripture says that God is slow to anger, which presents his righteous justice against sin as being heavily padlocked and hard to access. Scripture also, in contrast, presents God's mercy as having a hair trigger.[16] Notice how David says, "I confessed my transgressions to the Lord," and then it says, "and you made me wait in shame for days." No, it doesn't say that! David says, "I acknowledged my sin to you," and then it says, "and you made me walk around on bare feet while stepping on Legos." No, perceptive reader, it doesn't say that either! It does say this:

> I said, "I will confess my transgressions to the LORD,"
> and you forgave the iniquity of my sin. (Ps 32:5)

The forgiveness David experienced was immediate. As soon as he confessed his sin, he was forgiven. Remember the story of the prodigal son? He had turned to go back to his father's house but before he could even get a word out to offer to be a servant and earn his way back, his father embraced him, kissed him, and commanded that a party be thrown in celebration (Luke 15:20–24). The Father delights to show mercy, and he will delight to show mercy to any who confess their sin to him.

The forgiveness David experienced was full. It comes from the "infinite largeness" of God's heart and is given with "an inconceivable boundlessness"[17]:

> If there be any pardon with God, it is such as becomes Him to give. When He pardons, He will abundantly pardon. Go with your half-forgiveness, limited, conditional

of our devotion (see Luke 7:36–50).

16. The language of padlocked justice and hair-trigger mercy comes from Piper, *Pleasures of God*, 185.

17. Owen, *Works of John Owen*, 6:499.

pardons, with reserves and limitations, to the sons of men. It may be, it may become them; it is like themselves. That of God is absolute and perfect, before which our sins are as a cloud before the east wind and the rising sun. Hence he is said to do this work with his whole heart and his whole soul . . . freely, bountifully, largely to indulge and forgive unto us our sins, and to "cast them into the depths of the sea" (Micah 7:19).[18]

The forgiveness David experienced was free. Neither our repentance in general, nor confession in particular, is the ground, or reason, for our forgiveness. Neither are our promises to do better next time, nor do our commitments to be more spiritual manipulate or coerce God into granting forgiveness. Instead, God freely and joyfully grants us forgiveness based on his mercy alone in light of the work of Christ alone. This is the reason why, when David confessed or when we confess, we can experience the same forgiveness that is immediate, free, and full.

Selah

While the meaning of the word "Selah" at the end of many verses in the psalms, including the end of the verse we've studied in this chapter, remains uncertain, Hebrew scholar Derek Kidner suggests "pause" as a possible meaning.[19] This pause was more than likely either a pause in the music—a kind of interlude—or an opportunity for musicians to shift to different instruments. Either way, it gave the listeners an opportunity to consider in more depth what was just spoken or sung.

That is what we are invited to do at the end of this verse. Pause. David isn't only confessing personally, but he's also inviting us in to see his confession as a model that we ourselves can use when we find ourselves needing to confess sin. It's a model of refusing to hide and coming to the throne of grace boldly in our time of need. It's also a verse that motivates. We pause to consider

---

18. Owen, *Works of John Owen*, 6:499–500, 502.
19. Kidner, *Psalms 1–72*, 36–37.

the immediacy and fullness of forgiveness that David experienced so that we too might confess and experience the same thing.

Chapter Summary

Like Adam, we often hide because we think that if we confess sin, we will be condemned. Psalm 32 teaches us otherwise. The foundation of repentance is God's kindness. In his kindness, the Spirit helps us see that sin is more than actions that make us guilty, but also a condition of our hearts and a disposition to live for our own purposes. The Spirit, in kindness, also reveals the character of God. In revealing God's holiness, he deepens our conviction of sin; in revealing God's mercy he deepens conviction of our sin but also motivates us to confess it in light of the promises of Scripture that God will forgive. Thus, David expresses his repentance in a confession that is comprehensive, personal, and relational. In confessing, he is caught off guard. His heart expects some kind of condemnation or penance, but instead he experiences forgiveness that is immediate, free, and full. David's heart in this psalm is both a model and motivation for our own confession that we should pause to consider more deeply.

Study Questions

1. What has God done in your life not only to tell you about your sin, but also to show it to you?
2. What has God done in your life not only to tell you about his grace, but also to show it to you?
3. Knowing God's grace and forgiveness are immediate, free, and full when we confess, what do you need to confess right now?

6

An Inviting Heart

Therefore let everyone who is godly offer prayer to you at a time when you may be found; surely in the rush of great waters, they shall not reach him. You are a hiding place for me; you preserve me from trouble; you surround me with shouts of deliverance. Selah

PSALM 32:6–7

WHEN WE FIND AN experience exciting and fulfilling, our joy is not complete until someone else shares the same experience with us. When I was 17 years old, I drove from Indiana to Colorado for the first time because I wanted to see fields of corn in my rearview mirror while I drove toward majestic, snow-capped peaks in front of me. I'll never forget seeing the Colorado front range for the first time. My jaw remained open for days as I walked awestruck on rocky trails, surrounded by peaks that soared above 14,000 feet, encountering all kinds of new wildlife for the first time. Ever since then, I take a group of guys out there every summer to see the majesty and feel the experience of standing in the presence of such grandeur. These men, then, return home telling their families and friends in hopes that someday they can all go out there together.

They want those they love to see what they've seen, feel what they've felt, and experience what they've experienced.

In this section of Psalm 32, David is doing the same thing. He is practically aching for others to know and experience what he's come to know and experience from God. Here, he is continuing the upward orientation of his heart toward God in prayer, but he's also simultaneously turning his heart outward toward others. In this verse, he makes an invitation and then gives three reasons for the invitation: no condemnation, divine protection, and joyful celebration.

A Prayer and an Invitation for All

A Passionate Prayer

As you read the psalm, you sense that David's heart is catching on fire, and that is why he has a passionate desire for others to experience what he has experienced. An important word that you see here is "therefore." In light of the blessing he's received—the deep joy of experiencing the passionate and permanent favor of God—he wants others to experience the same thing. In light of the wrong path he took in trying to hide his sin, he wants others to avoid doing the same thing. In light of the unexpected abundance of grace he experienced when he was forgiven, he wants others to have the same experience and know his God. This is what he is praying for.

His prayer isn't just for a few people. He doesn't want to keep it to himself, nor only to his family, friends, or political or military advisors. Instead, as the king of Israel, recognizing God's desire to bless the nations through Israel (Gen 12:1–3), David says, "Therefore, let *everyone*. . ." He wants as many people as possible to experience the grace of God that he has experienced. He is prayerfully asking God to bring the blessedness mentioned in verses 1 and 2 of this psalm to many, many others.

An Inviting Heart

A Personal Invitation

Not only is this verse a passionate prayer of David but it's also a personal invitation. Anyone who sung this psalm in corporate worship or read it privately was being personally invited by the king of Israel himself to experience what he had experienced.

But for whom, in particular, is the invitation? David says, "everyone who is godly." You'll notice that David mentions no racial, socioeconomic, or political barriers. Everyone is invited. Not only that, he is inviting the godly. We need to be careful here and recognize that many of us have a preconception of what godly is that doesn't conform with what Scripture says. We might think the godly are those who focus almost completely on being doctrinally straight; however, our doctrine can be straight and our hearts can still be crooked. We might think the godly are those who strive heroically to be morally faithful; however, we can look moral on the outside and be spiritually adulterous on the inside. We might think the godly are those most committed to being socially involved; yet, we can care for the social outcasts while being a spiritual outcast ourselves. The list could go on and on. Thus, while doctrinal precision, moral faithfulness, and even social involvement are important aspects of the Christian life, they are not the essence of what it means to be godly.

The godly of Psalm 32 are those who, first and ironically, recognize clearly how ungodly they actually are. They recognize not only their natural, creaturely dependence on God as their Creator, but they also recognize the fundamental fallenness of their hearts apart from God's mercy. Recognizing both their creatureliness and fallenness, the godly rely completely on God for his saving and transforming grace. The godly of this verse, then, know this recognition and reliance at their core. For those who feel the weight and burden of their sin and have come to know they cannot rely on their own strength or wisdom, David offers them, offers you, a formal invitation.

It still remains for us to understand the purpose of David's invitation. He is passionately inviting others into the presence of

God himself through prayer. In the Old Testament, David and others could pray anywhere and be heard by God; however, the most intimate access to God was through the temple courts. Israelites could pray in the court of the temple, but only priests could go into the holy place and only the high priest could enter the Holy of Holies, and only then once a year. The New Testament, in light of the work of Christ, will joyfully declare that by faith, all believers have access to God's holy presence anywhere and at any time. This is so often heard within the walls of the church that we often lose the sense of what a staggering claim it is that we have access to God's presence in prayer (Rom 5:2; Heb 10:9).

Not only does prayer give us access to God's very presence, but it also means we have the intimacy of God's attention and the fullness of his affection. In Christ, God's face shines upon us; he delights to draw near to his children when they draw near to him. Infinite in essence, God can give each of his beloved adopted children his attention and affection when they pray and pour out their hearts.

Last, when and why can the godly pray to him? Here, David is further motivating our hearts by telling us that the time when God can be found is anytime we seek him. This is the same advice David will later give his son Solomon (1 Chr 28:9). Any time we genuinely seek God with our hearts through prayer, we will *always* find him. In fact, he's eager to be found by us (Ps 27:8; Jer 29:13). Do you believe that God is eager to be found by you? David wants you to.

The invitation has been given, yet David realizes that an invitation is often not enough. He must give some reasons for us to continue moving toward acceptance of his invitation to pray as he has. He gives three reasons: there is no condemnation, we can have divine protection, and we can be surrounded by joyful celebration.

AN INVITING HEART

Motivations to Receive the Invitation

No Condemnation

David's first motivational reason that he shares with anyone who sings or reads this psalm is "surely in the rush of great waters, they shall not reach him." This is curious language. What does he mean by "great waters" and how do his comments here comfort us?

When God rescued Israel from Egypt, their first enormous obstacle was the Red Sea. In his incomparable power, God separated the waters and Israel walked to the other side safely on dry ground. However, as soon as Egypt began to pursue Israel to force them to return to slavery, the waters returned and the Egyptians were destroyed. Reflecting on the Exodus, Psalm 77:19 states, "Your way was through the sea, your path through the great waters." Thus, the great waters were what Israel passed through safely and what fell on the Egyptians in judgment. Ezekiel uses the same image of great waters to convey the reality of judgment (Ezek 26:19), harkening back to the waters that covered the earth when Noah made his ark.

David is telling us that for those who confess their sin to God, no matter how deep and complex the struggle is, or how long it has gone on, there will be no condemnation. There may also be a reference to the chaos and randomness of life in using the words "great waters." We see, again, the same language used in Psalm 107:23 when describing sailors on the sea, a place that those in the ancient Near East saw as ruled by chaos. Yet God is the ruler of the great waters and can hush their raging (Ps 107:29). David, then, may also be seeking to encourage those whose faith leads them to pray, that the chaos of life will never completely overthrow their faith.

David goes an extra step and doesn't simply say, "In the rush of great waters, they shall not reach him." Instead, he says, "*Surely,* in the rush of great waters, they shall not reach him." There is a certainty and confidence that we can have in God's forgiving grace that David wants us to know. In David's day, there was the tabernacle and the sacrificial system. Because the animal sacrifice was slain and blood was shed on the mercy seat, Israelites could have confidence through faith that there was no condemnation for them.

However, the great waters of Noah's flood and of the exodus, and the sacrifices of the tabernacle and temple, all pointed forward to the person and work of Christ.[1] The reason that the great waters of judgment and condemnation will never fall on those who look to Christ by faith is because the great waters did fall on Christ at Calvary. All of the justice we deserved for our sin fell on him. In light of this, we can have the confident and comforting assurance that God will always shower us with forgiving mercy when we seek him in prayer. "There is therefore now no condemnation for those who are in Christ Jesus" (Rom 8:1).

Divine Protection

The psalms have an incredible amount of references to refuges and strong towers. Part of the implication of these images and metaphors is that the human heart, your heart, is always looking somewhere or to someone to protect us from the chaos and dangers of life. Sadly, Israel often sought military refuge in Egypt from other strong nations, rather than trusting their God (Isa 30:2). They also often sought refuge from the dangers of drought and infertility in Baal worship. In our age, we can make Netflix a refuge from boredom, fashion and dieting as a refuge from shame, or a thousand other idols that we look to for protection from our dangerous and fallen world. In Psalm 32, David uses the language of a "hiding place," a location where we are safe from what endangers us. Interestingly, David went from hiding *from* God to hiding *in* God.[2]

Due to the serpentine poison of sin that has been in our bloodstream ever since Adam's fall in Genesis 3, one of our first impulses when we sin is to hide from God. David even admits that he did this in verses 3 and 4 of this psalm. We hide because the law

---

1. See how Paul says that this psalm points to Christ's work in Romans 4:6–8.

2. This helpful insight is from my friend, George Sigalas, in a personal conversation on July 7th, 2018.

and our conscience tell us that we're guilty and can only expect a response of anger, with an anticipated penalty of condemnation. We hide because we feel shame, fearing rejection, followed by ostracism and abandonment.[3] Either way, whether we feel guilt or shame or both, the heart's tendency apart from grace is to hide from God.

In 2005, Brennan Hawkins, an eleven-year-old Boy Scout at the time, momentarily walked off the trail from his scout squad and got lost in the mountains of Utah. For the next four days, Brennan wandered the terrain and trails alone, trying to survive. When rescuers finally found him, he was alive but severely dehydrated.

Why did it take so long to find him? Every time he saw a volunteer rescuer on the trail calling his name, he would hide.

Why would Brennan hide from the very people who were trying to rescue him, especially in his deteriorating condition in the mountains? He later told reporters that his mother told him to never talk to strangers and that he was afraid someone would steal him. "Brennan was so concerned about being abducted by people who were trying to rescue him that he almost starved to death."[4]

This is exactly what Adam and David did, and every sinner after them naturally does: "And he said, "I heard the sound of you in the garden, and I was afraid, because I was naked, *and I hid myself,*"" (Gen 3:10, emphasis mine). The rescuing God came looking for Adam, but Adam was afraid and hid from God. David did the same and so do we.

David, however, knows that he no longer needs to hide from God. He has experienced God's blessing (vv. 1–2) and forgiveness (v. 5), and realizes that his only hope is to come out of hiding and move toward the God who is calling his name. Just as God asked Adam, "Where are you?" so he also asked David, and asks us when we sin, "Where are you?"

This question is not God's need for information; he's omniscient and knows all things, even the depths of our hearts (Rom 8:27). Instead, the question is acting as an invitation to come into

---

3. See especially Stump, *Wandering in Darkness,* 143.
4. This story is told in Twenge, *Generation Me,* 135.

the open, to the wide-open fields of God's heart where the sweet fruit of mercy grows, to the wide-open embrace of the Father where the tender touch of grace is felt.

David is motivating those who have sinned—no matter how consistently, deeply, and rebelliously—to come out of hiding. *The safest place in the world* after we've sinned is running into the presence of God with a heart that doesn't hide what happened, but openly confesses it, trusting in the grace of the Father's forgiveness.

Next, David elaborates even more on how God protects him and will protect those who pray to the Lord: "You preserve me from trouble." A crucial teaching of Scripture is that God's people persevere in faith and grace because God preserves them. While it's not an easy thing to hear, this means that everyone who reads this psalm is inherently weak and needs preserving because we cannot preserve ourselves.

In our weakness, God often preserves us from external troubles. Countless times every day God preserves us from numerous troubles that could fall into our path. This doesn't mean that God preserves us from ever going through difficult circumstances, but that because of his common grace, our world and our lives are not as dark and difficult as they could be.

Even more so, in our weakness, God preserves us from the internal troubles of spiritual trials. Again, this doesn't mean that we won't go through internal struggles, but it does mean that God will preserve our faith in whatever circumstances we find ourselves. This is clearly seen in the situation where Peter denied Jesus three times. Prior to Peter's actual denial Jesus says, "but I have prayed for you that your faith may not fail. And when you have turned again, strengthen your brothers" (Luke 22:32).

Peter's faith was deeply challenged, but it didn't fail—not because Peter was strong, but because Jesus was faithful. Notice that Jesus is so confident in God's preserving grace in Peter's life that he says, "*when* you have turned again, strengthen your brothers." Not if, but when. And Peter did exactly what Jesus said, he strengthened the brothers in his first epistle by telling believers that their

An Inviting Heart

faith, in the midst of various "fiery trials," was being guarded by God's power (1 Pet 1:5-6), just like his was when he denied Jesus.

The second motivation to receive David's invitation to prayer is that God can be our hiding place and that we are safe when we run to him. The third is experiencing joyful celebration.

Joyful Celebration

World War II lasted a little over five years and saw the total death toll rise to over 70 million people. When the war was finally declared over, 8,000 people per minute and half a million people per hour poured into Times Square in New York City. Eventually 2 million people stood in the Square, singing and celebrating so loudly that it could be heard for tens of miles around, and leaving five inches of ticker-tape covering dozens of city blocks. These shouts were in celebration of the Allied powers delivering Europe and the world from the murderous tyranny of the Axis powers of Germany, Italy, and Japan.

While David's battle in Psalm 32 hadn't been with other nations, it had been with a sinful reality in his heart driven by no less tyranny than the Axis powers. This sin had held him in such guilt and bondage that he did not have the power in himself to bring about deliverance. Himself the warrior-king of Israel, David needed another warrior to rescue him. And that is what he celebrates in this verse. These shouts of deliverance were in light of God delivering David from the deception, guilt, and power of sin.

This joyful celebration is rooted in deliverance from sin's deception. When David went astray, and when we leave the home of our Father for the far country of sin, we always do so because sin disguises itself as something good and pleasurable for us to enjoy. However, like camouflage used by armed forces around the world, its intent is to deceive in order to destroy. David fell for this deception and he couldn't deliver himself. What Psalm 32 celebrates, then, is that God has opened David's eyes to see sin for what it really is: a pathway to death (Rom 6:23). However, seeing sin clearly is only the beginning.

Not only does grace joyfully deliver us from sin's deception, but it also delivers us from sin's guilt. We often try to deliver ourselves from the grip of guilt by making promises and commitments to no longer fail or to add on spiritual acts like reading our Bible more, attending church more, or praying . . . more. Yet none of these things are capable of quieting the guilt that we have in our conscience and heart.

The only thing that can deliver David, or us, from sin's guilt is the shedding of blood (Heb 9:22). The Warrior God who delivered David from sin's guilt is the same God who would powerfully defeat sin and death through the weakness of the cross. As Michael Horton has said, "Jesus embraced the cross precisely as a king embraces a scepter."[5] The cross is the instrument that David's Warrior Lord eventually wielded to deliver him and us from sin's guilt.

Grace also delivers by breaking sin's power. Paul, in Romans, says that gentiles and Jews are under the power of sin. It's not enough to simply be forgiven, we must be freed from sin's power. This is precisely what the gospel does because it is both the power of God for salvation and for our growth in grace (Rom 1:16). Now, though sin's presence remains, the Spirit dwelling within our heart gives us strength to live for God and die to sin.

It's striking to notice that David isn't the one shouting. Instead, he says, "*You* surround *me* with shouts of deliverance." It's as if David is saying, "When I confessed my sin to the Lord, instead of hearing angry shouts that shamed me for what I did, I heard my Warrior God joyfully shout that I had been delivered, by his powerful right hand, from sin's deception, guilt, and power!"

Conclusion

David has given you a formal invitation to turn back to God in prayer. He motivates you with grace upon grace to return to a Savior who will surround you with shouts of deliverance. Will you

---

5. Horton, *Lord and Servant*, 254.

accept the invitation and seek God in prayer during a time when he may be found?

I hope you will.

Chapter Summary

In this verse, David says a prayer and gives an invitation for all. His passionate desire and prayer is for everyone to experience the free and full forgiveness that God eagerly gives. Thus, he offers a personal invitation to the godly, those who recognize their need and rely on God's grace, to seek God in prayer because God delights to be found by sinners. David follows his invitation for sinners to pray with three motivations. First, he motivates with the comforting assurance of no condemnation. Second, he motivates with the promise of divine protection. Sinners don't need to hide from God, but can hide *in* God, not only from external troubles but also amidst internal trials and temptations. Last, David motivates with the description of joyful celebration. God himself shouts for joy because he delivers sinners from the deception, guilt, and power of sin.

Study Questions

1. How does your conception of godly differ from the one in this psalm?

2. Do you have assurance that the "great waters" of God's justice will not reach you because you are in Christ by faith? If not, look to Christ by faith and ask the Spirit to give you this confident assurance in God's love.

3. Have you ever had such an experience of God's extravagant grace that you had to tell someone else in order for your joy to be complete? What is the most important takeaway from these verses for you that you might share with a friend?

7

A Wise Heart

I will instruct you and teach you in the way you should go; I will counsel you with my eye upon you. Be not like a horse or a mule, without understanding, which must be curbed with bit and bridle, or it will not stay near you. Many are the sorrows of the wicked, but steadfast love surrounds the one who trusts in the LORD.

PSALM 32:8–10

IN 2017, A WEST Coast company raised millions of dollars to begin something that has become something of an online sensation. It's called "Master Class." These brief, online courses enable you to learn from those who are considered the best in their fields. You can learn movie directing from Steven Spielberg, Ron Howard, or Martin Scorsese. You can learn acting from Samuel L. Jackson, singing from Christina Aguilera, or writing from Malcolm Gladwell. If you're into sports, Serena Williams teaches a course on tennis and Steph Curry teaches a course on basketball. In basically any field, they have courses from "The Masters."

In Psalm 32, David is giving us a Master Class in Grace. However, there's a difference between this and the online courses. He is not necessarily considered a master, but he has been mastered by grace. If anything, grace has taught David and now David is willing to teach us. It may not be the course that the masses sign up for, but for those who have been overcome by sin and constantly struggle with it, it will be exactly what we need.

A Counselor for the Way

From early church fathers all the way to current counseling practices, it's hard to guide someone into terrain where you yourself have not gone. In this section, David isn't simply declaring that he read some books at a school, knows some theories about addressing pathologies, and can now expertly hand down advice from on high. If David did have a PhD it was in waywardness. Thus, having received forgiveness and instruction from the Lord, he now turns to come alongside fellow sinners and counsel them with what he has painfully, personally, and gratefully learned.[1] His vulnerable counsel is insightful, directional, personal, and he desires to be present with those he guides.

Insightful

Notice the language David uses in verse 8—"instruct," "teach," "counsel." Each of these words show that David has learned a significant amount and gained deep insight in his wandering from God and in his return to God. He has gained insight into the human heart—how deceitful sin is, how hardened our hearts can become, the strategies we use to cover sin, and so on. He has

---

1. There is some debate as to whether David or God is speaking in verse 8. One could point to Psalm 16:7, 143:8, Isaiah 48:17, and Jeremiah 42:3. These all use similar language to this verse and speak of God doing the counseling. However, Psalm 32 is a psalm of confession very similar to Psalm 51, where in verse 13 David declares that, having experienced God's grace, he will now turn to teach transgressors the way of the Lord. I think there is evidence for either reading, but will primarily focus on David as the counselor here. Yet ultimately, God also counsels us with his eye on us, which we will see in a moment.

gained insight into the heart of God—how extravagantly gracious he is, what a loving Father he is, and the lengths he will go to in order to restore us back to him. Those who give the most insightful, penetrating counsel are those who have been given the painful gift of self-knowledge as well as the joyful revelation of what the heart and character of God are like, especially when we've failed so big and fallen so far.

Directional

David's counsel to others will not simply be a counsel of affirmation. He doesn't counsel us to trust in ourselves and realize how incredible we are, nor is he politely making some suggestions that we are free to follow or not, depending on our preferences. Instead, in verse 8, he talks about "the *way* you *should* go." He is giving bold and clear direction. There is a way and we should go in that way. Before we expect David to bust out a "5 Steps for Returning Prodigals" curriculum, we must realize, however, that "the way" in the New Testament is not first and foremost a list of principles to live by. When Jesus, the Son of David, taught and instructed others, he said that he himself was "the way" (John 14:6). All healthy, genuinely transformative counsel begins and ends with Jesus. At the same time, David will also have some practical steps to offer that we'll discuss below. Yet it bears repeating that gospel-centered counseling will both ground our hope of recovery in Jesus and give directions to move in as we are empowered by God's grace.

Now, if you choose to take a Master Class online, it can only take you so far. It can be insightful. It can be directional. But you're still only looking at a computer screen. Susan Dynarski, a professor of education, public policy, and economics at the University of Michigan, writes in a *New York Times* article that online education is helpful only for a certain group of students: accomplished learners. Less proficient and "academically challenged students need a classroom with a teacher's support," to genuinely thrive.[2] In other

---

2. Dynarski, "Online Courses," para. 7.

words, the most helpful teaching and counsel is the kind that is both personal—geared specifically toward the struggling student—and where the teacher is actually present. That is precisely what David wants to offer, even as the king of Israel. He longs to come alongside others and personally help them in the midst of their battles with sin. And we are *all* spiritual strugglers.

Personal

In verse 8, David uses the pronoun "you" five times. He uses it again in verse 9 for a total of six times in two verses. This counsel, then, is intimately personal. When God counsels us through his word, it is personal because he knows us exhaustively and speaks to us personally. When others come alongside us to counsel us, the best counsel is personal. Because of the security we have in the gospel, we've allowed someone to know our story, our strengths, our weaknesses, our struggles, our successes, and especially our sins. The best gospel counsel comes from those who know their own heart, God's heart, and your heart.

Present

God's counsel to us from his word comes with his presence, through the Spirit. David's counsel to sinners comes with insight, direction, and personal involvement, but even more closely with his presence, "I will counsel you with my eye upon you." This is the promise of spending time together, evaluating circumstances, decisions, habits, and patterns. This is a promise for the power of friendship. David is not content with inviting you to listen to his conference talk and then get on a plane to go home. Instead, he invites you to spend time with him. He wants to be near enough to be helpful. As we struggle with sin in community, we must allow a few others to be close enough friends that they can see how we respond to the different seasons of life, watch how we engage the various spheres of our life, and offer gospel help along the way.

Gospel Brokenness

The Way You Shouldn't Go

David is now going to give you some explicit encouragement to head in a certain direction. If understood in light of the whole Psalm, I think David is vulnerably opening his heart to say, "This is who I was. This is what I was doing. Learn from my sinful wandering." I think there are at least three sinful tendencies that are present in each beating heart that David is telling us to be aware of.

The Way of Self-Reliance

First, David is warning you not to be reliant on your own power. In Scripture, horses are portrayed as exceedingly powerful. Thus, when David says "Don't be like a horse," he isn't saying "Beware of the temptation to walk on all fours, neighing out loud, and scaring your neighbors with your totally strange behavior." He is saying, "Do not live life trusting in your own strength" (see Ps 20:7; Isa 31:1). Later, David will say that God's steadfast love surrounds those who trust in the Lord. This implies that relying on our own strength implicitly reveals that we don't trust God. It's looking at life and victoriously saying "I got this," or desperately believing that "I have to make this work." It's entering into the battle with sin saying, "I have to try harder and do more." *Sola bootstrapa* (by my bootstraps alone), believe it or not, was not a battle cry of the Reformation. Rely on your own strength and you'll eventually find out how weak you are.

The Way of Selfish Impulses

Second, David is counseling you not to be driven by your selfish impulses. Horses and mules have to be "curbed with bit and bridle" precisely because they don't naturally want to submit to the will of another. They are "without understanding" and therefore rather than think about what they are doing, they simply do what they want. Like the sheep of Isaiah 53:6, their deepest drive is to "go their own way." This is embedded in our everyday culture as we drive down the road seeing signs, listening to podcasts, or reading articles that give advice like "You be you," "Have it your own way," "Express yourself," *ad infinitum*. The very desires we're told to indulge are the ones David is counseling us to deny and kill.

The Way of an Impersonal Heart

Last, David is urging you against developing an impersonal heart. These animals are not only impulsive, but the only way they will stay near you is if you force them through coercion ("bit and bridle") or if you can help them get something they want. Otherwise, they "will not stay near you." The corruption and corrosion of sin in our hearts leads us increasingly on a path that, whether knowingly or not, sees others simply as objects that will help us get what we want or obstacles that will hinder us getting what we desire. Like David, our hearts do not stay near our heavenly Father when sin has convinced us he won't give us what we really want.

Relying on our own power, living to indulge our selfish impulses, and treating others impersonally may seem right or natural to us, but it's a pathway that Proverbs says ends in death (Prov 14:12; 16:25). David is here confirming what Asaph says in a later psalm—sin dehumanizes us, making us more like animals (Ps 73:22) than images of God.

Consequences of the Way

There are, understandably, consequences of living this way.

Personal Sorrows

David says, "many are the sorrows of the wicked." Yes, wicked means people like Hitler, but it also describes the heart when it pursues its own purposes in its own power, regardless of others. Notice, though, that it isn't simply some sorrows, but *many*. Blaise Pascal has said that the reason we don't want to be alone with ourselves is because we'd be forced to realize how sad and empty we actually are.[3] To avoid this, we pursue endless diversions. But sorrow is the result when we turn toward sin and away from the One who is life and joy (Ps 16:9–11).

Spiritual sorrows are part of these "many sorrows" that David mentions. Unrepentant sin devastates our communion with God and our assurance of his love. While we can never lose our union with Christ because it's founded on his perfect work, our communion with him can be greatly disrupted. Our desire for prayer deadens. Our passion for the word dries up. Our hunger for hearing the proclamation of the gospel in corporate worship becomes a bore. All of this will cause us to lose the sweet assurance of God's love that he deeply desires that we have.

Relational Sorrows

There are also relational consequences to our sin that lead to many more sorrows. Whether or not we are aware of it, sin hardens our hearts not only to God but also to others. Perhaps we become increasingly impatient with those closest to us. Maybe we become more secretive and aloof from others. We definitely begin to slack in our desire to get together with other believers because we might feel conviction or they might love us enough to gently and wisely confront us. We may convince ourselves that whatever sin we're engaging in is no big deal, but eventually others around us feel the weight of our waywardness in one form or another. Sin makes us increasingly selfish and isolated, both of which bring sorrow on a straight path to our heart.

Denying Our Sin and Sorrows

Every person is born with the natural ability to teach a Master Class. However, the one we teach is a Master Class in Denial. We can hear David's exhortation to not be self-reliant, act on selfish

---

3. Kreeft, *Christianity among Modern Pagans*, 172.

impulses, or make relationships simply functional, and we can say, "That doesn't describe me, I'm definitely not like that." This is where Scrooge can help us because he thought the same way. In Charles Dickens's novel *A Christmas Carol*, the first ghost shows Scrooge his past, especially places where he had significantly failed and also where he had terribly hurt others. Scrooge regularly cries out in forceful tones to be removed from the dream, that he couldn't bear looking at what he had done wrong, and that he wanted to be shown no more. In one final gasp Scrooge yells, "No more! I don't wish to see it! Show me no more!"[4]

However, the ghost of Christmas past, Dickens writes, "forced him to observe"[5] what had been done. Scrooge thinks the ghost is cruel, delighting to torture him, but as the story unfolds, we see that the visit of the various ghosts comes with the kind intention of changing Scrooge's heart. If we are reading Psalm 32 with a psalm-shaped heart, we'll invite the Spirit to expose the ways our hearts are like horses and mules. It is a mercy of God when he shatters our denial and forces us to observe the condition of our hearts and the consequences of our ways.

The Way You Should Go

If the way we shouldn't go is marked by a lack of trust that believes God isn't good, doesn't give good things, and doesn't do good things for us and therefore we have to make life work on our own, the first step on the way we should go is marked by movement toward trusting in God.

Move Toward God in Trust

"Steadfast love surrounds the one who trusts in the LORD." Trust knows that God *is* good, that he *gives* good things to us, and that he is always *doing* good for us. If David knew God's goodness, how

---

4. Dickens, *Christmas Carol*, 36.
5. Dickens, *Christmas Carol*, 36.

much more do we know the good heart of God after he gave his Son for us at Calvary?

Sometimes, when believers lack tust in God's goodness, we might find our hearts saying, "I'm surrounded by disappointment." Maybe, "I'm surrounded by sadness," or "I'm surrounded by incompetent people at work." It could be that, in your mind, you're surrounded by whiney kids, fair-weather friends, and all kinds of things that make you frustrated or angry. Perhaps, however, you've missed something as you surveyed the landscape around you.

Seeing His Steadfast Love

Most who are in the military or police force have trained significantly for something called situational awareness. They have a sense of what surrounds them at all times. They see and notice things the average person wouldn't see or notice because they've been trained to be situationally aware. In Psalm 32, David is doing just that—training us to be situationally aware. To use military language, David is training us to answer the questions of situational awareness:

"What is at your 12 o'clock, right in front of you?" the drill sergeant asks.

David trains you to see and then say, "the steadfast love of the Lord."

"What is at your 3 o'clock, to your right?"

You look again, it's still the steadfast love of the Lord.

"What is at your 6 o'clock, behind you?"

It's becoming clearer now, the steadfast love of the Lord.

You get the picture. All around, you are surrounded by the steadfast love of the Lord. Some of us have trouble seeing that steadfast love, but the Master Class of Grace teaches us to be situationally aware, helping us to see it everywhere we might look.

What is five minutes in front of you? God's love.

What is five years in front of you? God's love.

What is fifteen years behind you? God's love.

There are painful realities that rightly bring grief, tears, and agonizing sorrow that often blurs our ability to see two feet in front of us. While these things bring genuine grief, it's important to remember the word David uses here for God's love. Specifically, it is steadfast. This is God's *hesed*, or his faithfulness to his covenant promises. I like to think of it as his passionate commitment to keep his promises no matter what the cost. Incredibly, being faithful to his covenant promises would eventually mean sending Christ to Calvary. Here, Jesus not only paid for our sin, but also purchased for us as a gift the very trust we need in order to look to him by faith. Thus, David is saying that grace teaches us to know, through trusting God, that his steadfast love surrounds us at every moment, and always will.

In sum, David tells us that the way we should go is in the direction, first, of trusting God's goodness, and then, second, allowing grace to equip the eyes of your heart to see the steadfast love of the Lord that surrounds you at every moment, in every place, and in every sphere and season of life.

What This Means for You

God's intention in giving us Scripture in general and Psalm 32 in particular is that his word would shape the very fabric of our hearts. These verses encourage us to *acknowledge* that we've lived in self-reliant and selfish ways. This plays out in a multitude of varieties but each of our hearts go down these foolish roads and we must be aware of them and vulnerably confess them.

We can also *approach* Christ in our time of need, just like David did. Sin often convinces us that we cannot approach God because we're dirty and we've done wrong. Yet our ability to approach God isn't based on who we are or what we've done, but on who Christ is and what he has done. The book of Hebrews doesn't say, "Let us then hesitantly approach God's throne of justice, terrified as to whether he will give us ten thousand hours of time-out in the corner." Instead, the book of Hebrews states, "Let us then with confidence draw near to the throne of grace, that we may receive mercy and find grace to help in time of need" (Heb 4:16). Don't come hesitantly, instead, approach his throne confidently in Christ, yet humbly acknowledging your sin and your need for mercy.

Last, empowered by the Spirit, we *avoid* the foolish way of sin and instead walk on the better path of trusting in God which leads to incredible joy. Like the song of the sirens in Homer's *Iliad*, sin calls to us to enjoy its pleasures and walk down its path, only to destroy us. Most of us, however, try to fight sin like Ulysses did as his fleet went past. He has his crew put wax in their ears, tie him to the mast, and promise to refuse his demands to take him to the sirens as he's overcome by their sweet voices. Jason, on the other hand, has a better tactic. He brought Orpheus with him, the greatest musician in Greece. As he approached the sirens, he didn't tie himself to the mast or put wax in his ears, he simply told Orpheus to play music and they all made it by safely. He fought the enticement of a sinful pleasure, with the enjoyment of a greater pleasure. We, too, must fight the fleeting pleasure of sin (Heb 11:25) with the greater pleasure of knowing the heart of God in the music of the gospel.

Mastered by Grace

David had taken and then taught a Master Class in Grace. He gave counsel that was insightful, directional, and personal, and he desired to be present with those he would lead and counsel. However, as a mere human king, he eventually died. When Peter preached in the book of Acts, he said:

> Brothers, I may say to you with confidence about the patriarch David that he both died and was buried, and his tomb is with us to this day. (Acts 2:29)

However, the Son of David, Jesus Christ, rose from the grave and sits on the heavenly throne, sending his Spirit as our Comforter and Counselor (see Acts 2:30–36). Though David was *an* author of this psalm, God is *the* Author of this psalm and now, Christ, through the Spirit, gives you counsel that is deeply insightful, graciously directional, and intimately personal, with a vow to always be present with you in your struggles against sin.

During the holidays, the Master Class company often has a deal called "Take One, Give One." In other words, take a class, and gift a class to a close friend. I encourage you to take this course in grace from David and ultimately from Christ. Learn from his life. Learn from his heart. Like David, you won't become a master at grace, but your heart can be mastered by grace. And remember, grace is never to be hoarded, but passed along—just like David is sharing with you in this psalm. You, too, can have a wise heart.

Chapter Summary

Having been mastered by grace, David now teaches a Master Class in grace for those willing to sit at his feet and learn. His insightful, directional, personal, and present counsel will point you on the way toward Jesus. Negatively, he warns our hearts to avoid the way characterized by relying on our own power, enslaved by our selfish impulses, and relating to others in an impersonal way. This way only leads to many spiritual and relational sorrows. Positively, the way we should go is quite simple—trust God and realize that you are always surrounded with his steadfast love. To heighten our appreciation for God's amazing grace, we realize that even this trust in God is a gift from God. Therefore, we acknowledge our waywardness, approach Christ in our time of need, and avoid the foolish path of sin.

Study Questions

1. Who is someone in your life that has counseled you in a meaningful way and why did you appreciate your counsel from them?

2. In what specific ways or areas of your life is your heart like a horse or donkey?

3. How might your posture toward life change if you recognized you were surrounded by the steadfast love of the Lord?

8

A Joyful Heart

Be glad in the LORD, and rejoice, O righteous, and shout for joy, all you upright in heart!

PSALM 32:11

As WORLD WAR II was drawing to a close in Europe, the Allies were beginning to find concentration camps and free the prisoners. In one situation they came upon a German train that was headed to a death camp. Knowing the Allies were coming, the Germans were trying to eradicate as many prisoners as possible. If you were put on those trains, you knew all too well what was coming . . . unless someone more powerful came to the rescue.

While we have many pictures of concentration camp survivors *after* the liberations, we have few pictures of the exact moment the liberation occurred. In one instance, however, we have a picture of *the precise moment* the liberation occurred. The train was interrupted by American tanks and jeeps. There were a few shots fired but the Germans immediately surrendered. The doors to the train were opened and prisoners flooded out. One of the most famous pictures of the war was taken at this time by a soldier—a picture of a mom and her daughter holding hands, walking away from the train, while women in the background lifted their hands in the air, ecstatic with joy.

A young boy, fourteen years old, who would later become a medical doctor, was on that train. Describing the scene, he said, "The joy that seized us at the sight of the American tanks is indescribable. Suddenly from [being viewed as] nonhuman slaves, *we were transformed into free people. It was very thrilling, unforgettable.* . . . There was an outburst of joy that is hard to describe."[1]

The Way of Joy

In the previous chapter, we saw that David counseled believers to go in a certain way. Two of those ways were to trust in God and allow God's grace to show us that we're surrounded by his steadfast love. In this final verse of the psalm, David is continuing his Master Class of Grace and encouraging us in the way we should go. This third and final way that David counsels us in is to move toward the way of joy.

This way of joy that he speaks of is unexpected because it is so counterintuitive to those outside and inside the church. As a church planter, I've had many conversations with people who have never stepped foot inside a church and have a deep assumption that if they turn to Christ in repentance and faith and become involved in church life, it means nothing but a future of monotonous, joyless, rigorous routine. Sadly, many make this assumption because it's exactly what they've seen in family members or friends that are involved in evangelical churches—a lack of joy.

Some believers inside the church also make assumptions that go against the way of joy. Christianity is, in their minds, about orthodoxy and orthopraxis, making sure that we believe the right things and obey the right commands. While these aspects of claiming faith are true and essential, they miss an integral aspect of our lives—our emotions. Many believers are "suspicious of

---

1. Aderet, "Holocaust Train," para. 17 (emphasis mine). See also Rozell, *Train Near Magdeburg*.

A Joyful Heart

emotions in general" and "think that maturity is largely a matter of suppressing, if not eradicating, the emotions."[2] This mentality misses an essential link between orthodoxy (right belief) and orthopraxis (right actions)—namely, orthopathos (right emotions). This is especially seen at the ground level when repentance is up for discussion as it becomes increasingly evident that many see repentance as the need to *only* feel grief, sorrow, and regret over our sin, rather than *also* experiencing the joy of forgiveness and drawing near again to God.

The way of joy, then, isn't optional to the Christian life, it is essential. In fact, Scripture says that "the joy of the Lord" is to be our strength (Neh 8:10). Joy is one of the deepest and most fundamental drivers in the entirety of the Christian life.[3] In the psalms, joy is commanded and expressed for a variety of reasons. Believers should find joy in God's protection of them (5:11; 63:7), his provisions for them (65:12–13), his powerful reign over all things (47:1; 96:12), the salvation he brings (20:5; 51:12), his defeat of our enemies (27:6; 68:3; 81:1), and especially his intimate yet majestic presence (16:11; 21:6; 43:4; 84:2).

Thus, at the end of Psalm 32, David commands us to "Rejoice," to "be glad," and "shout for joy." David began with pursuing joy in the sins, transgressions, and iniquities that he mentions in the first couple of verses. Rather than joy, it led him into total exhaustion, deep shame, and "many sorrows." His grieving over this season of sin is ending with an explosion of joy as his heart is restored to fellowship with God. As Bryan Chapell states, "Repentance that renews precious fellowship with our incomparably wonderful God ultimately furthers our joy. Just as we cannot enter into true repentance without sorrow for our guilt, we cannot emerge from true repentance without joy for our release from shame."[4]

Joy is an essential aspect of the Christian life in general and of repentance in particular.

---

2. Roberts, *Spiritual Emotions*, 15.
3. See especially Piper, *Desiring God*.
4. Chapell, *Holiness by Grace*, 88.

Cultivating Joy

Remember the comment from the fourteen-year-old boy on the train when they had been rescued? "There was an outburst of joy that was hard to describe" as the prisoners were freed from their traumatic near-death experience. Those people didn't need to be told to feel joy; it was an intuitive, visceral response as their circumstances dramatically changed in an instant.

In his internationally best-selling, award-winning book *Emotional Intelligence*, Daniel Goleman describes two kinds of emotional responses. The first is what he calls the "fast-response"[5] which is experienced through immediate perception. In this situation, the experience of the emotion comes before thoughtful reflection. Think about when your team wins a close game or when someone surprises you with an unexpected trip to your favorite place to eat—you don't have to think about feeling joy, it's automatic! Some who reads Psalm 32 and hears about God's extravagant grace for prodigal sinners and their heart—like the boy in the train—instantly explodes with grateful joy in such a gracious God. They feel God's blessing—the deep joy of possessing and experiencing God's permanent and passionate favor—and rejoice; they sense him near as their hiding place and they are glad; they can see themselves surrounded by his steadfast love and they shout for joy. It is automatic. Deepened reflection on the grace described in this psalm will only continue to enflame and enlarge the joy that already exists inside our heart.

The second way to respond emotionally is what Goleman calls the "slow-response"[6] which comes more through reflective thought. In this response there is time given to extended reflection and only after focused attention for a duration of time do we begin to feel the emotion. In this scenario, thoughtful reflection comes before experiencing the emotion.[7]

---

5. Goleman, *Emotional Intelligence*, 293.
6. Goleman, *Emotional Intelligence*, 293.
7. Goleman, *Emotional Intelligence*, 293.

A JOYFUL HEART

Some will read Psalm 32 and read right over the end of the psalm and its call for joy and thus not feel the emotion of joy. For those like this, the psalm is not blasting you with blame or scouring you with shame, but sweetly inviting you—in love—to give thoughtful reflection to the truths of grace until your heart, which was once broken by sin, is broken into by a joy that is inexpressible and full of glory (1 Pet 1:9).

To enter more deeply into the joy commanded in Psalm 32, honest self-reflection and a healthy season of meditation on the words of this psalm will help. In Hosea 14, when God himself is calling Israel to return, he gives them the words they should use in their return (v. 2). God is doing the same thing in Psalm 32. The words of this psalm call for honest self-reflection that takes the general comments of David and explores the patterns and particularities of our own heart. Questions help us in this exploration: What specific sin, iniquity, or transgression have I committed and how do I try to hide it? In what ways has God pursued me to help me uncover what I've tried to hide? Have I, in light of the certainty of God's mercy, confessed openly to God and maybe to a trusted friend, the sins that I am struggling with? What aspects of the gospel speak specifically and most meaningfully to my soul right now? God delights to give us a broken and contrite spirit when we ask, and the more broken and shattered for our sin we feel, the more joy we'll know when we experience the healing balm of the gospel.

Meditation will also help in the cultivation of joy. Dennis Johnson and Elyse Fitzpatrick, in their book *Counsel from the Cross*, encourage believers to pursue the changing or deepening of their emotions by changing their core beliefs and the thoughts that continually fill their minds.[8] As has been mentioned in previous chapters, Psalm 32 reminds us that God is more gracious than our hearts often believe. He blesses sinners with eternal favor and infinite love. He showers transgressors with abounding mercy and incomprehensible grace. These truths must, by faith, be drilled

---

8. Fitzpatrick and Johnson, *Counsel from the Cross*, 129–50.

deeper and deeper into our hearts in order to anchor our joy in the person and work of Jesus Christ.

The Depth of Joy

Emotions are an essential aspect of our lives and play an important role in our following Jesus and responding to the good news of the gospel. Over time, they can also be cultivated and deepened so that we respond appropriately to biblical truths and life's circumstances. Emotions are also useful because they reveal what we most deeply cherish and love, value and treasure.

I firmly believe that every human being struggles with rooting their deepest joy in good circumstances. I'm joyful when the weather is perfect, when my wife is attentive to every word I speak and laughs at every joke I tell, when my kids obey everything I say with a smile on their faces, when the church I pastor is growing, and when my book becomes a *New York Times* bestseller. In other words, we each have a kingdom that we've designed according to our own desires, and our joy comes only when *our* kingdom comes.

The devastating aspect of this, however, is that it makes my joy tenuous and temporary. My joy will be tenuous, or weak, because it can easily be taken away by a little rain, a cranky kid, or a little problem in the church. Things that are relatively small can enormously impact my experience of joy. It will also make my joy temporary, lasting only as long as my circumstances hold up and my kingdom holds sway. These circumstantial joys are legitimate if enjoyed just as they are—circumstantial. It is when they become more to us—ultimate—that we enter the danger zone.

Believers also wrestle against sinful joys. Sin wouldn't attract us if we saw it for what it really is—a heart-corrupting, relationship-polluting, conscious-callousing, guilt-staining rebellion. Instead, it paints itself up with camouflage, enticing us to experience the joys and pleasures it has to offer (Heb 11:24–25). Sin always drives our heart to cry out, "More!" and never to contentedly say "Enough," precisely because it cannot deliver on its promises of joy.

More than circumstantial joys, and in opposition to sinful joys, the Spirit empowers believers to root their joy most deeply in the character and grace of God. Notice how David says, "Be glad *in the LORD.*" When LORD is capitalized in our Bibles it's always a reference to God's special covenant name, YHWH. This is not some general god who lives "up there," and who is not really involved with or concerned about the world. Instead, this is YHWH, the Creator of all things and the Redeemer of Israel, who is intimately involved in the world and passionately cares for his people. If David exploded with joy while considering the LORD as he revealed himself in the Old Testament, how much more should believers rejoice after the life, death, and resurrection of the Lord Jesus Christ in the character and grace of God!

This is the deepest anchor for our joy. Sinful pleasures are corrupting and circumstantial joys come and go, but the joy of the Lord remains forever. In an earlier psalm, David says that the height of joy in common grace pales in comparison to the joy of knowing God: "You have put more joy in my heart than they have when their grain and wine abound" (Ps 4:7). This image of deeply rooted joy is wonderfully captured by Tolkien when he describes the wizard Gandalf. If you looked at his face you might initially only see "lines of care and sorrow," but if you looked a little more carefully you would perceive "that under all there was a great joy: a fountain of mirth enough to set a kingdom laughing, were it to gush forth."[9] Believers, more than anyone else, should feel the weight and grief of a world shattered by sin; they should weep at the guilt and corruption that sin has caused in their own hearts and the hearts of others around them; yet, their strongest, deepest, and clearest note should be the note of joy.

Joy and Gospel Brokenness

While sorrow for sin is an essential aspect of biblical repentance, Calvin warns that "we must remember to exercise restraint, lest

---

9. Tolkien, *Return of the King,* 742.

sorrow engulf us." Driving believers to despair over sin has been a strategic ploy utilized by Satan to tear the fabric of believers' faith ever since the beginning.[10] Joy is also an essential mark of repentance that is healthy and gospel centered. Jack Miller, who spoke often on the great need for ever-deepening repentance in the church and in believers, says that "the sure mark of authentic repentance is boldness and joyous enthusiasm for the things of God."[11] Sin turns our hearts into a desert wasteland, but "the more you deepen your repentance the more room you have in your heart for rivers of living waters."[12] Can you imagine being in the desert, with no water in sight, no shade from the searing heat, and then a rock begins to gush with cool, crisp, clear water? That same joy is experienced in the heart of any sinner who genuinely turns from sin to the God who describes himself as "the fountain of living waters" (Jer 2:13; 1 Cor 10:4).

In this verse of Psalm 32, this kind of sorrowful yet joyful repentance is to characterize the life of "the righteous" and the "upright in heart." It's easy to think of the righteous primarily as people who are known for being passionate about worship, committed to spiritual disciplines, and kind to everyone. However, if whatever external righteousness we have is not generated by faith, it is considered by God to be a "polluted garment" (see Isa 64:6). Instead, "the righteous" in the psalms are "those who are bound to God by true faith in terms of the covenant."[13] In other words, the truly righteous realize that faith precedes and is the root for the fruit of faithfulness. In Psalm 32, a man who sinned, tried to cover it up, and eventually confessed is righteous, not because of what he did, but because of his faith in God's promise to provide a Messiah.

The "upright in heart" mentioned in this verse are those who, being given a new heart by God's grace, desire integrity between their outward behavior and inner posture. They know how twisted, dark, and deceitful their hearts can be, but long for their hearts to

---

10. Calvin, *Institutes*, 3.3.15
11. Miller, *Repentance and the 20th Century Man*, 25.
12 Miller, *Repentance and the 20th Century Man*. 54.
13. Godfrey, *Learning to Love the Psalms*, 17.

conform more and more to the character of their heavenly Father and loving Savior. They want to walk in the way of anchoring their deepest joy in God.

The Joy of Coming Home

This psalm now begins to come to a close. It portrays a prodigal sinner who had left the safety, security, abundance, fellowship, and joy of home for the far country of sin. All of us are prodigals with our own common and unique temptations toward and failings of sin. Perhaps you're more like the rebellious and reckless younger brother who is convinced that joy doesn't reside in the father's presence but over the horizon away from home. Perhaps you're more like the religious and responsible older brother who enjoys the gifts the father gives but not the father who gives them, viewing him as a harsh, demanding taskmaster.

Either way, this psalm is calling and inviting all sinners to the joy of coming home. Once we have "come to our senses" (see Luke 15:17) and realized the "many sorrows" (Ps 32:10) that sin brings, we realize that God is the *guide to our joy*. When he speaks to us through his word, he is guiding us along paths that lead to joy. He is also the *giver of joy* as he reminds us of all the gifts he gives us throughout our days and throughout our lives. Ultimately, though, God himself is the *source* of joy:

> You make known to me the path of life; in your presence there is fullness of joy; at your right hand are pleasures forevermore. (Ps 16:11)

If God is the guide to and the giver and source of our joy, then we as believers should be known as the *people of joy*. This joy is a delightful fruit that the Spirit works in our hearts (Gal 5:22) and characterizes the inhabitants of the kingdom of God (Rom 14:17).

If you knew that upon your return from sin and turning toward the Father that he would "celebrate and be glad" (Luke 15:32) while also filling you with a joy infinitely greater than any sin could ever deliver, wouldn't you turn around and go back home?

The strong love, forgiving grace, and deep joy of the Father's heart are waiting for you!

Chapter Summary

David's counsel is that believers should not only walk in the ways of trusting in God and seeing his steadfast love surrounding us, but also in the way of joy. This way is unexpected and counterintuitive as we expect the way of repentance, or gospel brokenness, to be the way only of joyless obedience. Emotions, especially the emotion of joy, are an important aspect of the Christian life. This joy can be immediately experienced in response to the good news of forgiveness or it can be cultivated through self-reflection and gospel meditation. The depth of our joy is also an important indicator of what we value most. As forgiven sinners, we still struggle with rooting our deepest joy in good circumstances or sinful pleasures. The Spirit, in contrast, helps us to anchor our deepest joy in the character and grace of God who is our guide, the giver and source of our joy. Believers, then, should be marked as the people of joy and be motivated to return whenever we've wandered from the Father's presence.

Study Questions

1. How does gospel brokenness change our normal understanding of what the outcome of repentance is?

2. Where are the places you tend to root your deepest joy in and what steps can you take to root your joy most deeply in the heart of God?

3. Do you immediately respond with a joyful heart when you hear the news of forgiveness and grace? If so, why do you think you do? If not, why do you think you don't?

9

The Path Towards Deep Joy
Gospel Brokenness

JOHN OWEN, COMMENTING ON the heart of King David, said:

> Under the Old Testament none loved God more than he; none was loved of God more than he. The paths of faith and love wherein he walked are unto the most of us like the way of an eagle in the air—too high and hard for us. Yet to this very day do the cries of this man after God's own heart sound in our ears. Sometimes he complains of broken bones, sometimes of drowning depths, sometimes of waves and water-spouts, sometimes of wounds and diseases, sometimes of wrath and the sorrows of hell; everywhere of his sins, the burden and trouble of them. Some of the occasions of his depths, darkness, entanglements, and distresses, we all know. As no man had more grace than he, so none is a greater instance of the power of sin, and the effects of its guilt upon the conscience, than he.[1]

Throughout this book, King David has been our guide on the unexpected path toward joy. We've seen his struggles with sin, his season of trying to deal with it in his own power, and the cry of his

---

1. Owen, *Works of John Owen*, 6:333.

heart in utter helplessness that God and God alone could rescue him and heal his wayward heart.

This chapter takes up the various themes that have been developed from Psalm 32 and puts them all into five basic statements about gospel brokenness. These statements are somewhat of a summary of the teachings of men who have been my guides on the journey of repentance. Along the way I've learned from Calvin's *Institutes,* John Owen's *Mortification of Sin* and his *Exposition of Psalm 130,* Richard Sibbes's *The Returning Backslider,* Thomas Watson's *Repentance, and* John Calqhoun's *Repentance,* along with the specific works on repentance by both Jack Miller and Sinclair Ferguson.

Many of these men made some kind of distinction between what was often labeled "legal repentance" and "evangelical repentance." They saw this distinction not as some ivory tower theology that has no daily ramifications for ordinary believers, but as essential for the spiritual vitality and growth of everyone who calls on the name of Christ.

Picture yourself at a juncture in the road. You're experiencing conviction over some sin in your life and there are two possible paths. One is the way of legal repentance and the other is the way of gospel brokenness; one is the way that leads to death, the other is the way that leads to life, joy, and peace. To help you know which way to take, you must know the contrasts between the two.

Two Possible Paths

The first contrast between false and true repentance has to do with its duration and source. False repentance is *a sporadic feeling of the heart as a result of guilt and discouragement.* This repentance is completely self-oriented, more concerned about eradicating a sense of guilt and discouragement than actually sinning against our heavenly Father. This feeling of guilt might be produced by God's law, our conscience, or simply feeling like we've let ourselves

The Path Towards Deep Joy

or others down in light of expectations. Yet simply being grieved by the guilt sin produces is not repentance.[2]

It is also self-sufficient, relying on our own power and resources to eradicate feelings of guilt.[3] Promises to do better next time are made, vows to no longer sin are spoken. At the core, however, is a reliance on our own power to grit through the struggle. However, if enough time passes or a season of not struggling with some specific sin occurs, one does not feel the need to repent much because the feeling of guilt has evaporated. This kind of repentance becomes increasingly sporadic as external behavior is modified and the sense of discouragement has waned—there is simply less to repent of now that behavior has been managed. As Sinclair Ferguson notes:

> What gives repentance power is not the *guilt* evoked by the Law alone (Rom 7:7), but the *grace* proclaimed to us only in the gospel of our Lord Jesus Christ. It is the kindness of God that leads to repentance.[4]

In contrast, true repentance—what we're calling gospel brokenness—is *a perpetual habit of the heart that is the result of the presence and power of the Spirit.* Gospel brokenness is not about self-sufficiency but Spirit-wrought dependence on God. In Scripture, the ability to turn from sin and toward God is itself a gift from God (Lam 5:21; Jer 17:14; Zech 12:10; Acts 10:44; 11:16–18).[5] The Spirit then exposes sin in our heart and life, enables us to see it (John 16:8), and empowers us to turn from it.

Because gospel brokenness is a gift and is wrought in us by the Spirit, it also is not something we do initially or periodically, but consistently and faithfully, until we see Jesus face-to-face. The "race of repentance," as Calvin called it, is to be run throughout

---

2. Sibbes, *Works of Richard Sibbes*, 2:256.
3. Sibbes, *Works of Richard Sibbes*, 2:259.
4. Ferguson, *Grace of Repentance*, 53 (emphasis his).
5. Watson, *Doctrine of Repentance*, 11–15; Miller, *Repentance and the 20th Century Man*, 42. Calvin, *Institutes*, 3.3.21.

our entire lives.[6] Even as we grow in the gospel, we are to grow more deeply in gospel brokenness as the Spirit increasingly reveals more of the darkness of our own sin and the brightness of God's abounding grace. Strikingly, growth in godliness actually deepens and increases repentance rather than decreasing it.

A second sharp contrast between false repentance and genuine gospel brokenness is their distinctive motivations. *False repentance is motivated by misery and fear.* It tends to view God as fiery, judgmental, and harsh, with his explosive anger hanging on a hair trigger.[7] Not convinced of his mercy but deeply assured of his anger, one does not desire to draw near, as you would likely get a slap in the face and a call to never come back.

Rather than receiving grace from a merciful God, this false repentance turns in a (conscious or unconscious) direction that tries to earn God's favor back by feeling guilty enough or miserable enough. There is a lack of certainty about God's mercy and the heart might think, "*Maybe* God will show mercy *if* I feel miserable enough." Sadly, one never knows how much felt misery is enough and never has the assurance of God's mercy. This motivation through misery and fear tragically fails in the end because it keeps the sinner away from the One who can actually help.[8]

Gospel brokenness is *motivated not by misery and fear but by the certainty of mercy by faith*. It is motivated less by the promises we make to amend our ways and more by the promises God has made to show forgiving and transforming mercy to those who ask (see 1 John 1:9). Rather than saying, "*Maybe* God will show mercy *if* I feel miserable enough," gospel brokenness says, "God *has* shown mercy to his people and to me in the past and promises that he *will* show mercy to those who run to him, therefore, I repent." This is Paul's approach in Romans when he tells us that it is God's kindness that leads us to repentance (2:4).

Faith helps us see with clarity the character of God. Rather than an oversized ogre who is more than happy to take you to task

---

6. Calvin, *Institutes*, 3.3.9. See also 3.3.2 for similar comments.
7. See Owen, *Works of John Owen*, 6:377.
8. Sibbes, *Works of Richard Sibbes*, 2:255.

over the smallest infraction, faith sees the clearest and most climactic expression of the Father's heart displayed in the person of Christ. By faith, the Spirit enables our hearts to see the remedy for sin in Christ and receive the mercies which come from the Father through him. Faith uniquely strengthens this gospel brokenness because it grasps the reality of justification, giving us the freedom to see—rather than deny—the darkness and twisted depths of our sin, enabling us to confess it, receive forgiveness for it, and forsake it. Thus, as theologian John Murray has insightfully said, "Saving faith is permeated with repentance and repentance is permeated with faith."[9] Puritan Richard Sibbes helps us see that the end of repentance must be a coming to Christ for mercy:

> It is not sufficient for a wounded man to be sorry for his brawling and fighting, and to say, he will fight no more; but he must come to the surgeon to have his wounds stopped, dressed, and healed, or else it may cost him his life. So it is not enough to be humbled for sin, and to resolve against it. We shall relapse again, do what we can, unless we come under the wing of Christ, to be healed by his blood.[10]

The sorrow felt for sin is a third difference between false repentance and gospel brokenness. False repentance is *superficially saddened over the temporary consequences of sin*. There are a variety of subtle consequences that one might be disturbed by. Some sin may sadden our hearts because it goes against our self-image as someone who "shouldn't struggle with things like that," such as anger, impatience, or lust. Our sin may result in some kind of consequence for our relationships which displeases us. Perhaps someone saw us being unkind to a store clerk and now they've been distant or cold in their interactions with us. Maybe some kind of sinful relational pattern has kept us from getting a promotion at work or being a leader in the church. Whatever the case, the disappointment is not about the actual sin, but the specific consequences of it in our lives.

9. Murray, *Redemption Accomplished and Applied*, 119.
10. Sibbes, *Works of Richard Sibbes*, 2.256.

Gospel Brokenness

Yet if the sadness is actually over the sin rather than simply over its consequences, false repentance tends to be superficially sad. Why? Because, c'mon, what's the big deal? Life goes on, I'll deal with this issue, and we'll all continue moving in the same direction. False repentance loves to keep track of other people's sin, maximizing their guilt while minimizing our own. So, yes, I'm sad about the sin in my heart, but what's for dinner? Because false repentance isn't marked by faith, it fails to see sin for what it really is.

Gospel brokenness, however, *genuinely and deeply grieves the gravity and enormity of sin's guilt and deformity.* Gospel brokenness doesn't simply grieve the consequences of sin, but grieves for the One sinned against—our gracious and loving God (Ps 51:3–4). Faith sees the enormous guilt of sin in light of the law God, but it sees even more of its gravity in light of the love of God, especially as Jesus endures the agony of Gethsemane and the curse of Calvary. The law helps us see the guilt of sin, but the gospel helps us to see the cost of that guilt and the deformity of sin's depravity.

This is why Zechariah says that it is not when we look to the law, but when we look upon the One who was pierced for us, we will grieve (12:10). We haven't simply broken a law, but we've rebelled against the heart of a Father who gave his Son for us, a Savior who gave his life for us, and a Spirit who gave new life to us. Seeing sin clearly for what it is in light of the gospel, gospel brokenness grieves and hates sin for what it really is—rebellion against our loving Creator and Redeemer.[11] However, it is especially here that it is wise to listen to Calvin as he offers a caution amidst the grief of gospel brokenness, "we must remember to exercise restraint, lest sorrow engulf us."[12]

The remedy embraced and pursued is a fourth area of difference between false repentance and gospel brokenness. False repentance tends *to focus on external actions and embraces religious devotion as the remedy.* One focuses simply on what has been done rather than on where those actions are coming from. To review

---

11. For more on how the Spirit helps us grieve sin, see especially Owen, *Works of John Owen*, 6:368–72; Sibbes, *Works of Richard Sibbes*, 2:369–70.

12. Calvin, *Institutes*, 3.3.15.

from a previous chapter, unbelief tends to convince us that sin is manageable and that we are capable of dealing with it in our own strength. Thus, all we need is an exercise regimen to tell us what to do and in a short amount of time, we'll be back on track.

Gospel brokenness, because it *focuses more on our internal condition than our external actions*, joyfully embraces the only remedy capable of actually dealing with our problem—the forgiving, cleansing, and empowering grace of God. What is most deeply important is the realignment of our worship, not the management of our behavior. Whatever "fruit sins" we have in our lives are coming from "root sins" in our heart (Luke 6:43–45).

False repentance and gospel brokenness also part ways in the way faithfulness to God is pursued. In false repentance, *the heart tries to obey but remains secretly convinced of sin's ability to satisfy*. Obedience is experienced as a joyless burden and sin retains its appeal as joy-filled pleasure. God is still viewed as harsh and narrow, not wanting us to experience things that give us joy. In this person's heart, obedience is a burden, and sin remains the real joy.

Gospel brokenness is *confident in God's forgiving and enabling grace and seeks comprehensive faithfulness in all of life*. The gospel shapes our heart to view sin as a burden and obedience as a joy. How? Through the work of Christ, we've been adopted into our Father's family and are children of God. We've seen, tasted, and experienced the gracious fatherhood of God and know how merciful he is and how wise his commands are. His ways are not to fence us off from joy, but the fence within which we experience the greatest joys in fellowship with him. As a good Father, he has also given us the Spirit to empower our faithfulness to him in every sphere and season of life. Rather than viewing sin as something that's manageable, gospel brokenness relies on the miracle of grace to move toward God and away from sin.

In sum, false repentance is *the sad path toward spiritual death*. It is a sporadic feeling of guilt, motivated by fear, saddened by sin's consequences, focused on external actions, and reliant on promises and commitments to do better in order to change and be accepted by God. Once we've failed again on our journey to please the God we see as quickly angered, it will only be a matter of time before we walk toward the welcoming embrace of sin. It is a cycle, Paul says, that leads to death (2 Cor 7:10). Gospel brokenness, however, is *the necessary path toward life and joy*. This posture of heart realizes that we're a project under construction and God himself is the guarantor that it will one day be complete (Phil 1:6). The ground of God's mercy in our lives is the perfect and complete work of Christ, not the quality or quantity of our repentance or obedience. As we continue our struggle with sin, we realize that our growth in grace is all of God's work, yet he works in us and through us that we might continually leave the lesser joys of sin for the greater joys of his glorious presence and plentiful grace.

Conclusion

Oscar Wilde, most famous for his play "The Importance of Being Earnest" and his book *A Portrait of Dorian Gray*, is an example of someone who sought ultimate joy apart from God and yet only found sorrow. In jail, toward the end of his life, he wrote the following:

> I let myself be lured into long spells of senseless and sensual ease . . . Tired of being on the heights, I deliberately went to the depths in the search for new sensation . . . Desire, at the end, was a malady, or a madness, or both. I grew careless of the lives of others. I took pleasure where it pleased me, and passed on. I forgot that every little action of the common day makes or unmakes character, and that therefore what one has done in the secret chamber one has some day to cry aloud on the housetop. *I ceased to be lord over myself. I was no longer the captain of my soul, and did not know it. I allowed pleasure to dominate me. I ended in horrible disgrace.*

He later goes on to say,

> I wanted to eat of the fruit of all the trees in the garden of the world, and that I was going out into the world with that passion in my soul. And so, indeed, I went out, and

The Path Towards Deep Joy

so I lived. My only mistake was that I confined myself so exclusively to the trees of what seemed to me the sunlit side of the garden, and shunned the other side for its shadow and its gloom. Failure, disgrace, poverty, sorrow, despair, suffering, tears even, the broken words that come from lips in pain, remorse that makes one walk on thorns, conscience that condemns, self-abasement that punishes, the misery that puts ashes on its head, the anguish that chooses sack-cloth for its raiment and into its own drink puts gall—all these were things of which I was afraid. And as I had determined to know nothing of them, I was forced to taste each of them in turn, to feed on them, to have for a season, indeed, no other food at all.[13]

While these are both longer passages, they are worth pondering. Seeking only the little "j" joys that this world had to offer, he missed the ultimate "J" Joy that comes from knowing God. Refusing to feel sorrow or despair, that is precisely where his story ends.

I do not know Wilde's heart, especially in his last days. However, I do know that Psalm 32 could have met him deep in his soul. David had felt a similar crushing sorrow as Wilde, but instead David turned toward Joy when he turned toward God. You turn toward Joy when you turn toward God.

That is what gospel brokenness is all about. It is a turning from moldy food to the Bread of Life, it is turning from darkness to the Son of righteousness, it is turning from the far country back to the home of the Father, it is turning from broken cisterns that can hold no water to the One who is Living Waters, it is turning from death to life, bondage to freedom, guilt to forgiveness, sorrow to joy.

Chapter Summary

Building on the work of pastors and theologians of the past, gospel brokenness seeks to know and navigate the turning point between

---

13. Wilde, *De Profundis*, 6, 9 (emphasis mine).

legal repentance, which leads to death, and evangelical repentance, which leads to life and joy. Gospel brokenness differs from legal repentance in its duration and source, its motivation, its depth of sorrow, the remedy embraced, and the way faithfulness is pursued.

Study Questions

1. How did your heart respond as you read the quotes from Oscar Wilde?
2. Are there ways in which you practice "legal repentance?" What are they?
3. Why is "evangelical repentance" or "gospel brokenness" more inviting to a thirsty soul?

You can read more of Clay's work by visiting his website www.deephearted.org or you can email him at claywerner@gmail.com.

Bibliography

Aderet, Ofer. "The Holocaust Train That Led Jews to Freedom Instead of Death." https://www.haaretz.com/world-news/europe/.premium.MAGAZINE-the-holocaust-train-that-led-jews-to-freedom-instead-of-death-1.5446799.

Agassi, Andre. *Open: An Autobiography.* New York: Random House, 2010.

Anderson, Nick. "Johns Hopkins Mistakenly Says 'Yes' to Hundreds of Rejected Students." https://www.washingtonpost.com/local/education/johns-hopkins-mistakenly-says-yes-to-hundreds-of-rejected-applicants.html.

Augustine. *Confessions.* New York, Penguin, 1961.

Beck, Eckardt. "The Love Canal Tragedy." https://archive.epa.gov/epa/aboutepa/love-canal-tragedy.html.

Brooks, David. "Love and Merit." https://www.nytimes.com/2015/04/24/opinion/david-brooks-love-and-merit.html.

Brown, Steve. *A Scandalous Freedom: The Radical Nature of the Gospel.* West Monroe, LA: Howard, 2004.

Bunyan, John. *The Pilgrim's Progress.* Mineola, NY: Dover, 2003.

Calqohoun, John. *Repentance.* Carlisle, PA: Banner of Truth, 2010.

Calvin, John. *The Institutes of Christian Religion.* Library of Christian Classics. Edited by J. T. McNiell. Translated by F. L. Battles. Philadelphia: Westminster, 1960.

Carson, D. A. *The Gospel According to John.* PNTC. Grand Rapids: Eerdmans, 1991.

Chapell, Bryan. *Holiness by Grace: Delighting in the Joy That is Our Strength.* Wheaton, IL: Crossway, 2011.

Clowney, Edmund P. *Christian Meditation: What the Bible Says about Meditation and Spiritual Exercises.* Vancouver: Regent College Press, 1979.

Craigie, Peter C., and Marvin E. Tate. *Psalms 1–50.* World Biblical Commentary. Nashville: Thomas Nelson, 2004.

Dickens, Charles. *A Christmas Carol.* New York: Bantam, 1965.

Dynarski, Susan. "Online Courses are Harming the Students Who Need the Most Help." https://www.nytimes.com/2018/01/19/business/online-courses-are-harming-the-students-who-need-the-most-help.html.

Bibliography

Elkins, James. "How Long Does it Take to Look at a Painting?" https://www.huffingtonpost.com/james-elkins/how-long-does-it-take-to-_b_779946.html.
Ferguson, Sinclair. *The Grace of Repentance.* Wheaton, IL: Crossway, 2010.
Fitzpatrick, Elyse M., and Dennis. E. Johnson. *Counsel from the Cross: Connecting Broken People to the Love of Christ.* Wheaton, IL: Crossway, 2009.
Futato, Mark. *Transformed by Praise: The Purpose and Message of the Psalms.* Phillipsburg, PA: P & R, 2002.
Gilkey, Langdon. *Naming the Whirlwind: The Renewal of God-language.* Indianapolis: Bobbs-Merrill, 1969.
———. *Shantung Compound: The Story of Men and Women Under Pressure.* New York: HarperOne, 1975.
Godfrey, Robert W. *Learning to Love the Psalms.* Orlando: Reformation Trust, 2017.
Goleman, Daniel. *Emotional Intelligence: Why it Matters More Than IQ.* New York: Bantam, 1995.
———. *Focus: The Hidden Driver of Excellence.* New York: HarperCollins, 2013.
———. *Vital Lies, Simple Truths: The Psychology of Self-Deception.* New York: Simon and Schuster, 1986.
Guinness, Os. *God in the Dark: The Assurance of Faith Beyond the Shadow of Doubt.* Wheaton, IL: Crossway, 1996.
Haidt, Jonathan. *The Righteous Mind: Why Good People are Divided by Politics and Religion.* New York: Random House, 2013.
Hemingway, Ernest. *The Complete Short Stories of Ernest Hemingway.* New York: Simon and Schuster, 1987.
Horton, Michael. *Lord and Servant: A Covenant Christology.* Louisville: Westminster John Knox, 2005.
Hugo, Victor. *The Hunchback of Notre Dame.* Translated by A. L. Alger. New York: Dover Thrift, 2006.
Janz, Denis, and Sherry E. Jordon, eds. *A Reformation Reader: Primary Texts with Introductions, Augmented & Improved.* Minneapolis: Fortress, 2002.
Johnson, Eric L. "One Edge of a Two-Edged Sword: The Subversive Function of Scripture." *The Journal of Spiritual Formation* 9.1 (2016) 54–76.
Kegan, Robert, and Lisa Laskow Lahey. *An Everyone Culture: Becoming a Deliberately Developmental Organization.* Boston: Harvard Business, 2016.
Kidner. Derek. *Psalms 1–72: An Introduction and Commentary.* Tyndale Old Testament Commentaries. Downers Grove, IL: InterVarsity, 1973.
Kreeft, Peter. *Christianity among Modern Pagans: Pascal's Pensees Edited, Outlined, and Explained.* San Francisco: Ignatius, 1993.
Lewis, C. S. *God in the Dock.* Grand Rapids: Eerdmans, 2014.
Longman, Tremper. *How to Read the Psalms.* Downers Grove, IL: InterVarsity, 1988.

Bibliography

———. *Reading the Bible with Heart and Mind*. Colorado Springs: Navigators, 1997.
Miller, John C. *The Heart of a Servant Leader*. Edited by Barbara Miller Juliani. Phillipsburg, PA: Presbyterian and Reformed, 2004.
———. *Repentance and the 20th Century Man*. Fort Washington, PA: CLC, 2009.
Monagan, David, and David O. Williams. *Journey into the Heart: A Tale of Pioneering Doctors and Their Race to Transform Cardiovascular Medicine*. New York: Gotham, 2007.
Murray, John. *Redemption Accomplished and Applied*. Grand Rapids: Eerdmans, 2015.
Noble, Alan. *Disruptive Witness: Speaking Truth in a Distracted Age*. Downers Grove, IL: InterVarsity, 2018.
Owen, John. *The Works of John Owen*. 23 vols. Edited by William H. Goold. Carlisle, PA: Banner of Truth, 2010.
Packer, J. I. *Knowing God*. Downers Grove, IL: InterVarsity, 1993.
Pennington, Jonathan T. *The Sermon on the Mount and Human Flourishing: A Theological Commentary*. Grand Rapids: Baker, 2017.
Piper, John. *Desiring God*. Colorado Springs: Multnomah, 2011.
———. *The Pleasures of God: Meditations on God's Delight in Being God*. Colorado Springs: Multnomah, 2000.
Reeves, Michael. *Delighting in the Trinity: An Introduction to the Christian Faith*. Downers Grove, IL: InterVarsity, 2012.
Roberts, Robert C. *Spiritual Emotions: A Psychology of Christian Virtue*. Grand Rapids: Eerdmans, 2007.
Rozell, Matthew. *A Train Near Magdeburg: A Teacher's Journey into the Holocaust and the Reuniting of the Survivors and Liberators, 70 Years On*. Hartford, NY: Woodchuck Hollow, 2016.
Rutledge, Fleming. *The Crucifixion: Understanding the Death of Christ*. Grand Rapids: Eerdmans, 2015.
Sayers, Dorothy. *Letters to a Diminished Church: Passionate Arguments for the Relevance of Christian Doctrine*. Nashville: Thomas Nelson, 2004.
Scazzero, Peter. *The Emotionally Healthy Leader: How Transforming Your Inner Life Will Deeply Transform Your Church, Team, and the World*. Grand Rapids: Zondervan, 2015.
Sibbes, Richard. *The Works of Richard Sibbes*. 6 vols. Edited by Alexander B. Grosart. Carlisle, PA: Banner of Truth, 1983.
Smith, Scotty, and Steven Curtis Chapman. *Restoring Broken Things: What Happens When We Catch a Vision for the New World Jesus Is Creating*. Nashville: Thomas Nelson, 2005.
Stump, Eleonore. *Wandering in Darkness*. Oxford: Oxford University Press, 2010.
Thompson, Curt. *The Soul of Shame: Retelling the Stories We Believe about Ourselves*. Downers Grove, IL: InterVarsity, 2015.
Tolkien, J. R. R. *The Return of the King*. New York: Del Rey, 2012.

BIBLIOGRAPHY

Trosclair, Gary. "Self-Deception is Killing Us: Why Self-Awareness Matters." https://www.huffpost.com/entry/selfdeception-is-killing-_b_8294162.

Trueman, Carl. *Grace Alone: Salvation as a Gift from God.* Grand Rapids: Zondervan, 2017.

———. *Luther on the Christian Life: Cross and Freedom.* Wheaton, IL: Crossway, 2015.

Turkle, Sherry. *Reclaiming Conversation: The Power of Talk in a Digital Age.* New York: Penguin, 2015.

Twenge, Jean. *Generation Me.* New York: Simon and Schuster, 2006.

Wallace, David Foster. *This Is Water: Some Thoughts, Delivered on a Significant Occasion, about Living a Compassionate Life.* New York: Hachette, 2009.

Watson, Thomas. *The Doctrine of Repentance.* Carlisle, PA: Banner of Truth, 1988.

Welch, Edward T. *Shame Interrupted: How God Lifts the Pain of Worthlessness and Rejection.* Greensboro, NC: New Growth, 2012.

Wilde, Oscar. *De Profundis and Other Prison Writings.* Edited by Colm Toibin. London: Penguin, 2013.